Educating Disruptive Children

Placement and progress in
residential special schools for pupils with emotional
and behavioural difficulties

by Roger Grimshaw with David Berridge

The National Children's Bureau was esablished as a registered charity in 1963. Our purpose is to identify and promote the interests of all children and young people and to improve their status in a diverse society.

We work closely with professionals and policy makers to improve the lives of all children but especially young children, those affected by family instability, children with special needs or disabilities and those suffering the effects of poverty and deprivation.

We collect and disseminate information about children and promote good practice in children's services through research, policy and practice development, publications, seminars, training and an extensive library and information service.

The Bureau works in partnership with Children in Wales and Children in Scotland.

ISBN 1 874579 24 5

Published by the National Children's Bureau, 8 Wakley Street, London EC1V 7QE. Telephone 071 278 9441. Registered charity number 258825.

Typeset by Books Unlimited (Nottm), Rainworth, NG21 0JE

Printed by Biddles Ltd, Guildford

Press cutting on cover © The Telegraph plc, London 1993

Contents

List of tables

Foreword

The 1993 Education Act aims to achieve a level of intervention and support which will allow children to progress in mainstream school. But it acknowledges that 'where family support is lacking or inadequate, or family influence is damaging ... boarding away from home may be the only way for them to make progress.' (DFE Circ 9/94 DH LAC para 61)

Residential special schools have recently lived through difficult times. Placements have dropped as official policy has rightly sought to keep children in their home community and as local authorities have been beset by financial problems. In addition, the shocking revelations of abuse in a few schools have cast a cloud of suspicion over the rest. The new child protection procedures have meant that one professional group is now required to inspect another and, with different priorities and different levels of expertise, there have predictably been tensions. Yet these children above all others need the united support of all those who work with them. The Children Act and the 1993 Education Act are both concerned with children's rights; the right to be kept safe, the right to be properly educated. And both Acts are concerned to support and involve families wherever possible.

What is lacking is accurate and objective information on which joint multiprofessional policies can be based. The research recorded in this book begins to fill that gap. It shows up weaknesses, that placement in residential schools is haphazard, as much a matter of chance as of carefully assessed need. It shows that all schools need to have statutory supervision of their child protection procedures. It also shows strengths. As well as providing data about children at admission, it studied them for a year, and noted that change for the better was achieved, that many children and their families were significantly helped. It should be the forerunner of many more such enquiries.

Marion Bennathan,
Chair, Association of Workers for Children with Emotional and
Behavioural Difficulties

Acknowledgements

There was a very long period when it appeared doubtful whether this research would ever be started, never mind completed. In fact, David Berridge, then the Bureau's Research Director, spent the best part of five years on the task of obtaining financial backing for a project that had won approval from a range of practitioner and academic sources. Understandably the gratitude we express to the eventual funders of the research is particularly heartfelt. A generous financial contribution was made by the Nuffield Foundation, a liaison ably facilitated by Pat Thomas. Additional financial support was provided by the Hesley Group of Schools and the National Children's Home (now NCH Action for Children). Coming from sponsors of residential EBD schools, their contributions to this wholly independent project were particularly impressive. We must therefore give special thanks to the people instrumental in securing this vital support – Stephen Lloyd and Doug Pattison.

We were fortunate indeed to benefit from the cheerful and informed consultancies of Brahm Norwich, from the Institute of Education, University of London, who guided the project over methodological and statistical pitfalls. David Berridge was responsible for the original design of the project and supervised the work throughout. I would like to thank David in particular for helpful discussions about the extensive programme of fieldwork that I undertook; for his methodological advice; and for his eagle-eyed scrutiny of the wobbles and gaps in my prose!

Moving further afield, a sincere note of thanks is due to those dedicated staff of the schools that took part in the study, especially the Headteachers who were models of kindness as well as cooperation.

We need to express particularly grateful thanks to Philippa Stobbs, Marion Bennathan, Dan Gooch and Roger Bullock for their comments on drafts. Many others at various points took time to add to our knowledge of this wide subject. Vital support and assistance was given by Ebah Eshun, Kay Rufai, Fiona Blakemore, Samantha Jayaram, and colleagues in the Bureau's Libarary and Information Service.

As I close, let me add that the authors accept responsibility for errors in the text. Finally, but most importantly, I should like to thank the children and young people who are the subject of this book; I can only hope that their help and cooperation are adequately justified by the final product.

Roger Grimshaw

1. Introduction

Residential schooling holds a place in contemporary culture as a form of imaginary childhood, whether expressed in traditional boarding school tales or in contrasting accounts of progressive communities. Its appeal is largely due to the difference between childhood in a family home and a childhood where teachers and schoolmates form almost a separate social world, in surroundings often far removed from a familiar urban environment. In the space opened up between family and school, there is scope for the invention and speculation that fuels successful fiction. Attaining a more objective view of residential schooling can be far more challenging, since the sense of separateness has to be overcome by the research, without detracting from those unusual characteristics that drew our attention at the outset.

Doing justice to these distinctive and separate social worlds takes time, as well as patience and energy. But, above all, it requires a method of gathering and using information to answer specific questions. In this study of residential special schools for pupils with 'emotional and behavioural difficulties' (EBD), the questions surround key aspects of children's experience – referral and admission; the systematic practice of schooling; and a broad range of outcomes for children. The case studies in this book have been selected in order to shed light on the interconnections between these phases of a very complex process. The presentation of material in the chapters reflects the series of major questions which are dealt with. The purpose of this introduction is to set the scene for what follows by explaining why residential EBD schooling deserves greater objective scrutiny, especially at this time. In addition it outlines the reasoning which led to the choice of particular methods of investigation.

In England and Wales, the organisation of residential provision for children considered difficult or disruptive has been governed by a range of legal and administrative structures. Children deemed at risk of significant harm to their development because of the care they receive have been candidates for services made available by the social services departments of local authorities. These have included a range of 'community homes', some with educational facilities. Psychiatric units overseen by health authorities have also offered care for difficult and distressed children. But the supervision of residential special schooling has remained the general responsibility of local education authorities (LEAs) and the Department for Education; the LEAs have been bound by the provisions of the Education Act 1981 to assess children's 'special educational needs'. Access to special schools has, in principle, depended on obtaining a formal 'statement' of special educational need, following an assessment. The legislation on special education has adopted the term 'emotional and behavioural difficulties' to categorise various problems attributed to children. The present study concentrates, therefore, on a sector for which educational agencies have exercised primary responsibility.

Images of uncertainty

The public profile of residential EBD schools has risen recently, for reasons that are, to say the least, regrettable and unfortunate. Readers of the press are perhaps more likely to be aware of scandals and school closures than of the actual work undertaken by staff and children in typical schools. In the well-publicised case of Castle Hill, systematic abuse of children was subsequently identified (Ogden, 1992; Brannan and others, n.d.). Other problems have reached the headlines when an investigation has been launched concerning indiscipline or allegations of staff misbehaviour (Scherer, 1992). The question marks hanging over the schools have been similar to those affecting children's homes in the aftermath of Pindown, when a strict isolation regime was applied to vulnerable children with disastrous results (Levy and Kahan, 1991). Policy responses have been dictated by events that have gained publicity, such as the exposure of Crookham Court, which reinforced the case for new inspection regulations for all independent schools whether or not they were special schools. Attention to the daily work of schools appears much less evident. Hence the residential EBD schools have seemed to operate under a climate of suspicion which has been unrelieved by any visible attempt by government to evaluate their work fully and to settle their future. The closure, for financial reasons, of Peper Harow, which was long considered a flagship establishment among the 'therapeutic communities', has tended to reinforce the sense of malaise and uncertainty (Wilson, 1993).

A scarcity of research

This research was conducted at a time when the residential EBD sector was undergoing much negative publicity. Yet there was little evidence about current practice in what had previously been a hidden and arguably neglected area of services. A number of classic accounts (for example, Balbernie, 1966; Shaw, 1965) represent the work of 'pioneers' but obviously do not focus on the present. Studies of 'good practice' in special education for 'disturbed' children have charted the diversity of trends in approaches (Dawson, 1980; Wilson and Evans, 1980). But direct evidence about placement and progress has been hard to come by, with some notable exceptions (Roe, 1965; Lampen and Neill, 1985; Malek and Kerslake, 1989). At the same time, interest in school disruption, and in 'difficult' children more generally, has never ceased to hold public attention (DES, 1989).

The importance of improving EBD provision was identified as a priority in the Warnock report on special educational needs (DES, 1978). But, since then, curiously, it appears that we know less rather than more about what has happened. To illustrate this, the available evidence about the extent of the sector makes a useful starting point.

A question of numbers

The special schools have come to be divided administratively into the LEA sector, the independent sector, and the non-maintained (or charitable) sector. Regrettably, an official unified listing of residential EBD special schools in England and Wales does not seem to be readily available. A major survey of boarding provision identified 325 residential schools catering for behaviour difficulties in 1986-7 (Anderson and Morgan, 1987). In 1988, another survey built up a sampling frame of approximately 217 residential EBD schools (Smith and Thomas, 1992). A similar method based on the *Local Authorities directory* for 1987 obtained responses from 139 schools with residential provision, out of a total of 355 schools and units offering either day or residential provision for EBD (Cooper and others, 1991).

The study by Anderson and Morgan (1987) found 31 per cent of all special schools with boarding provision to be independent or non-maintained. Similarly, Cooper and others (1991) found that about a third of EBD schools and units were independent or non-maintained. Unfortunately, the survey by Smith and Thomas (1992) appears not to have covered non-maintained schools.

The resulting picture is distinctly inconclusive and gives little scope for a national overview capable of guiding management or policy: as we shall see further, it is impossible to be sure to what extent the residential EBD sector has increased or diminished.

Trends in 'statementing' under the Education Act 1981 tell us something about the numbers of children educated in different forms of provision. However, they do not include children in units for disruptive pupils, whose number was estimated in the middle of the decade to be about 7,000 (Ling and Davies, 1984). The rate of statementing has been increasing on average for all types of need (Lunt and Evans, 1991; HMI/Audit Commission, 1992a), but the proportion of children in special schools in general has been in decline.

In broad terms, there has been a reduction in the proportion of children in all special schools from 1.72 per cent in 1982 to 1.58 per cent in 1990 (Swann, 1991). However, the proportion of those children in maintained EBD schools seems to have remained stable recently, at between seven and nine per cent of the maintained special school population in the period from 1987 to 1992 (Audit Commission, personal communication). Figures for the non-maintained and independent sector continue to be elusive. A slow proportional decline, in line with the general trend, would seem to have taken place for the EBD special school population as a whole. In the Shire Counties, however, some proportional increase in the EBD special school population has been identified (Cliffe and Berridge, 1991). Without the official collection of statistics, a degree of uncertainty about national and local trends cannot be removed. This seems particularly unfortunate given, as we shall see, the potentially vulnerable nature of the pupil population.

In similar vein, a recent analysis of statementing rates, this time in largely urban areas, has indicated that EBD statements form a varying proportion of all statements. There is also evidence of complex variations among local authorities, between the number statemented and the numbers actually in EBD provision. Thus, not only does the general statemented group itself vary in its composition, there are differences in the specific use of statementing to deal with EBD. More informal provision may contain some pupils who, it is suggested, would in other authorities have received statements (Peagam, 1991). Examining children's referral documents gives an insight into the process by which pupils were statemented and how far these informal services had been used – a topic discussed in the next chapter.

Information about the residential EBD population itself can only be derived from estimates. Two sources are possible: an OPCS survey of disability in 'communal establishments' and a general survey of boarding school provision. The distribution of children with a behavioural disability was estimated from an OPCS national survey conducted between 1985 and 1988.

Table 1.1 Estimates of numbers of children with a behavioural disability in Great Britain, 1985-88

	Age groups	
	5–9	10–15
Private households	76000	110000
Communal establishments	533	4720

(from Bone and Meltzer, 1989)

This table is perhaps most useful as an indicator of the disparity between the estimated numbers in communal and in private homes. The greatest proportion of children considered difficult continued to live in ordinary households but there was a significant increase in the proportion of children accommodated elsewhere at the secondary stage. This survey of communal establishments was designed to address health problems and unfortunately excluded children who went home on most weekends. The picture of residential establishments is therefore incomplete.

The second and more comprehensive source of information is found in records of pupil boarding. Figures for England in 1983 represent the last official tally (using the superseded term 'maladjusted').

Table 1.2 Maladjusted pupils resident in boarding special schools and LEA boarding homes, England, 1983

Maintained	Non-maintained	Independent	LEA boarding homes	Total
6774	1145	4376	314	12609

(see Parker, 1988)

The national survey of Anderson and Morgan (1987) allows a reasonable estimate to be made of the numbers in England and Wales a few years later, though the categories are somewhat different.

Table 1.3   **Pupils at residential EBD special schools: Estimates: England and Wales, 1986–7**

	In county LEA		Out county LEA	Independent schools and homes	All children
Boys	Girls	Total			
4550	893	5443	375	5375	11193

(see Anderson and Morgan, 1987)

Taking into account the broader coverage of the later survey the difference in totals suggest some reduction in absolute pupil members. More recently, a similar view has been expressed by Pyke (1993). Another survey, however, as we saw earlier, points to some proportional increase in the shire counties (Cliffe and Berridge, 1991).

A leading provider of residential care for the disadvantaged

Evidently, it is not possible to be conclusive about trends in provision. However, the survey of Anderson and Morgan (1987) can be used as a baseline and general changes since that time can help form a current picture. After consultation with informed sources, it seems reasonable to suggest an estimated current population of 8,000 children in residential EBD schools. It would be ideal, of course, if official statistics were published; indeed it seems remarkable they are not. Nonetheless, the estimate appears to be the best available approximation to the actual figure.

The estimate takes on added interest and significance if trends in other residential provision are compared. For example, the number of children in local authority children's homes run by social services has decreased markedly in recent years, declining in fact to 1,000 **below** the estimated number in residential EBD schools. The number of children in specialist local authority community homes, such as those with educational facilities, stood recently at about 3,000. The residential EBD sector, therefore, appears to be to be a leading provider of residential care for disadvantaged children with difficulties at home and in school. Yet there is hardly any sign that current patterns have been adequately reflected in positive policy and management initiatives (Utting, 1992). Despite their importance, such changes have, surprisingly, not been the subject of public discussion and policy decision.

Leaving to one side the vexed question of numbers, it is essential now to show how concepts of 'problems' in childhood have altered, creating a very different set of evaluative criteria from those that may once have been applied in research.

The rise and fall of the 'maladjusted' child

A number of developments in special education have occurred that have changed the definition of emotional and behavioural problems. Historical studies have shown how charismatic individuals organised a variety of schools, catering for a wide range of difficulties (Bridgeland, 1971). A set of powerful forces progressively installed medical and psychiatric definitions of 'problem children' within the educational system. These came to influence the referral of children to special schools. Attempts were made to define difficulties in terms of 'maladjustment', which denoted a disturbance within the child for which treatment was appropriate.

This attempt to develop a coherent definition was not altogether successful and led to criticisms of what was termed a 'medical model'. Children's difficulties had been attributed to inner disturbances, rather than to outer adversities. Instead of this, a broader task was envisaged, attending more to the child's environment. A concept of 'special educational need' was produced, which looked beyond the children's health or disability to their actual educational needs. Classification of handicap was to be superseded in favour of individual prescription (DES, 1978).

In the rhetoric and practice of special education the concept of individual need remains primary (Malek and Kerslake, 1989). To focus solely on the individual, however, is to risk glossing over the relationships in which the child's behaviour occurs. In the psychology and sociology of education there has been a reorientation of attention towards the contexts and relationships in which children are defined as difficult or disorderly (Bowman, 1981; Gillham, 1981). The same reorientation has guided this research project. For this reason the research has given particular attention to the ways in which behaviour has been **interpreted**, whether at home or in mainstream and special schools.

Who defines the problem behaviour?

To talk of emotional and behavioural difficulties implies paying more attention to what we mean by a 'normal' childhood. Clearly, there is a degree of emotional stress and worrying behaviour in every child's history. What leads adults to perceive some feelings and behaviour as sufficiently disturbed to warrant acute concern? The idea of a normal childhood presupposes that some definition of normality can be arrived at, but this is not straightforward. One way is to look at the behaviours prohibited by law. While this gives a starting point, it hardly covers the full range or extent of problems that can be described as emotionally and behaviourally challenging. For example, surveys of teachers indicate that up to 40 per cent of children have been considered 'troublesome' (Docking, 1989). Clinicians have also attempted to chart the range of problems that parents and teachers perceive in children. The clinical approach is designed to put that process on a scientific footing by measuring the intensity and frequency of problems. Findings suggest that up to ten per cent of children show signs of clinical 'disorder' (Rutter and others, 1976). Though such rigour is useful, it leaves some assumptions insufficiently examined. In particular, it accords to teachers and parents the initial task of determining what appears to be a significant problem. It therefore tends to accept conventional assumptions about childhood in present day society, in which individual parents take responsibility for their own children, assisted by professionals, such as teachers in compulsory education.

For a realistic view of behaviour problems, we are obliged to recognise the influence of social processes by which some people define others as deviant (Tomlinson, 1982). By extension we have to see clinicians in their social role as authoritative interpreters of disturbance, adding a further layer to the common-sense definitions used by parents (Rutter, 1975). These points encouraged the development of questionnaires for the present study that drew on children's own self-assessments. With such considerations in mind it is worth examining what the conventional studies have told us about the development of behaviour problems, dealing primarily with families and schools, as well as pointing out other significant social influences.

Happy and unhappy families

The influence of the family on children's behaviour is widely acknowledged. However, the form and extent of family influence has been continually debated and reviewed. The idea that separation experiences in early childhood have generally had a sustained and irreversible effect on children has been found to be exaggerated (Rutter, 1972). The breakdown of marriages has been associated with a range of problems (Kiernan, 1992).

However, it has been shown by rigorous analysis that the more important factors were deprivation and family discord (Ferri, 1976; Rutter and Giller, 1983; Cherlin and others, 1991). Competent parents who offered a framework of consistency, control and esteem have been found to be more successful, especially when both parents enjoyed a positive relationship with each other and the child. Differences in family structure were less important (McCord, 1990). A focus on parental behaviour as such has seemed to represent a plausible hypothesis for understanding the behaviour of children.

Another finding also drew attention to parents' difficulties, by showing an association between childhood 'disorders' referred for clinical diagnosis and parents' physical and psychiatric condition (Rutter, 1966). However, this association applied only to a minority of the clinical population and has again been overshadowed in its effect on children by marital disharmony. Further analysis has suggested that the quality of relationship between psychiatric patients and their children has been the primary issue (Rutter and Madge, 1976).

However, concentration on the inner life of the family should not lead us to overlook a series of influences on adults that make child-rearing difficult. Psychiatric disorder in adults is itself often linked to social and personal stresses (Brown and Harris, 1978). Deprivation, as has been mentioned, also plays a significant part. The mother's role in this society can also be associated with a relatively high level of stress in women (Rutter and Quinton, 1977).

Families are influenced by wider cultural responses to social situations. There can be an appeal in the masculine connotations of some physical and manual work, which is reproduced in boys' resistance to school (Willis, 1977; Reid, 1986). Some children are drawn away from school by domestic responsibilities directly linked to parents' needs (Grimshaw and Pratt, 1985; Grunsell, 1980).

In such cases it would be unwise simply to invoke a clinical label and ignore the social meanings of behaviour disapproved by schools. Bringing schools more directly into the equation opens up a range of difficulties which schools can create for children, according to an impressive series of research studies.

The management of (mis)behaviour in school

Schools are run by adults for children, demanding a massive and disciplined commitment of time and attention. It is not surprising that the daily practice of teachers has a major impact, either for good or ill, on children's emotions and experience, and thereby on their conformity. The design of the environment and the curriculum play a part in this process, as do the specific ways in which teachers define and maintain order. The development of curriculum objectives influences the scope of discipline, creating new demands on children's concentration and skills. Allocation to a hierarchy of teaching groups carries the risk of reinforcing the negative assumptions of some children about their abilities and prospects (Hargreaves, 1967). Poorly designed curriculum programmes can sow the seeds of disaffection (Reid, 1986). Introducing a new national curriculum with a regime of testing carries further the process of challenging children, thus requiring a substantial investment of teachers' attention in the lowest achievers.

Furthermore, the disciplines of both school and home are influenced by the conditions in which activities take place. One condition is the availability of time and personal attention, which may be scarce not only in deprived and depressing homes but also in classrooms with overstrained teachers (Graham, 1986; Galloway and others, 1982). A pleasant school environment, predictably enough, contributes to better outcomes (Rutter and others, 1979).

Values and customs enter into the definition of social discipline. These, however, vary from group to group in scope or emphasis. In schools, they are translated into a latent curriculum, controlling sexuality, language and legitimate forms of address (Davies, 1984). Insolence to teachers, for example, has been found to be a major reason for exclusions from school (Galloway and others, 1982).

The maintenance of this order is woven into the fabric of daily interactions in schools, with very evident results. Teachers' assumptions about behaviour shape the way they respond to pupils, as they monitor instances of suspected or confirmed deviation. Portraits of particular children's idiosyncrasies are formed that may be unfair or unreliable (Hargreaves and others, 1975). At the same time children become aware of teachers' perspectives, both positive and negative. It has been shown that pupils' poor behaviour can be significantly amplified or moderated by the responses of teachers (Rutter and others, 1979; Reynolds and Sullivan, 1987). The use of special groups and measures for the disruptive forms part of this discretionary field of action. School organisation also patterns responses to disciplinary infractions, giving rise to sharply different rates of exclusion.

The importance of schooling in generating and modifying emotional and behavioural difficulties, therefore, can no longer be underestimated. It ranks alongside the home as a significant environment for children. These are not the only social factors, however, that need to be acknowledged. It is important to examine the social forces that impinge on particular sections of the school population, such as boys and girls, and minority ethnic groups.

There has, for example, been a preponderance of boys in both the general, and the specifically residential, EBD sector (HMI, 1989; Malek and Kerslake, 1989; Cooper and others, 1991). But the reasons for this are not straightforward. Some evidence points to a basic similarity between boys and girls in their school behaviour (Ford and others, 1982; Davies, 1984). However, there is also evidence that girls who pose difficulties are more obviously a minority of their sex, compared with similar boys (Davies, 1984). Girls' aggressive behaviour has also been found to be less frequently physical (Cairns and Cairns, 1992). Girls may be less often seen as challenging the social order of the school, and therefore may be subjected less frequently to attempts to remove them to EBD provision (Malcolm and Haddock, 1992). The significance of girls' under-representation deserved exploration in the present study and prompted the decision to include a range of coeducational schools.

The social framework which helps define difficult children is further illustrated by the body of evidence which shows the over-representation of children from minority ethnic groups in forms of EBD provision (Ford and others, 1982; Tomlinson, 1983; Cooper and others, 1991). It appears that children from minority ethnic groups are labelled as difficult in disproportionate numbers, resulting, for example, in a significantly higher rate of exclusion from schools (Nottinghamshire CC, 1990). Boys classified as black and African-Caribbean have been found to be the most heavily over-represented, compared with Asians, who are under-represented (Newth, 1986). Studies have shown teachers' perceptions of the culture and attitudes of black pupils to be inaccurate and unfair (Driver, 1981; Wright, 1986; Gillborn, 1990). The position of black people in the labour market has also been linked to school outcomes, indicating a pattern of institutionalised discrimination and disadvantage which schools have not sufficiently addressed. The experience of minority ethnic groups was therefore a significant focus of the research, especially as little was known about the residential population. However, one small scale study found a lower than expected proportion of children from minority ethnic groups, but noted once again the over-representation of children classified as 'Afro-Caribbean' (Gunaratnam and Berridge, 1990). An inconsistent picture of minority ethnic group placement varying among authorities emerged from a similar study of placements (Malek and Kerslake, 1989).

It should not be assumed that because schools and families influence children's behaviour they will agree in labelling an individual child as difficult (Mitchell and Shepherd, 1966; Rutter and others, 1970). Indeed, this theme is crucial in examining the statutory process of special needs assessment, where parents have had a recognised, if limited, role to play (Cornwell, 1987). In particular, a discrepancy between parents' and teachers' views has been noted for black children (Rutter and others, 1974 and 1975; Bagley, 1976). In addition to possible questions about racism in schools, there is a more general issue about whether teachers have been more sensitive to indicators of disruption and aggression than to quieter forms of unacceptable behaviour (Reid, 1986). The evidence of behaviour in school and at home has been central to the present study. Above all, we need to be aware of the combination of factors that leads to the singling out of certain children.

It is important to note that children designated as having behaviour difficulties also typically experience a range of other difficulties, in health and in learning (Rutter, 1975). It is the combination of stresses that is important not only in influencing the child but in making demands on parents and teachers. It becomes hard in these circumstances to single out one problem and to resolve it. Relationships with adults become fraught with persistent tension. The attractions of a special school placement are likely to increase because of the needs of adults – something very different from the needs of children.

Children also enter into their own social world which makes specific demands. Non-conformity with sections of the age group can reinforce the isolation of individual children and lead to the imposition of unpleasant labels. The complex social world of peer relations should not be underplayed. Its significance for children from minority ethnic groups, faced with racist language, has recently been thrown into sharp focus (Troyna and Hatcher, 1992; Keise, 1992). Where this web of social relationships among peers and with a range of adults comes under strain, the case for seeing a child as having particular difficulties, and as having special needs, would seem to be strengthened. The EBD label emerges from this nexus of experiences and relationships.

These various points have implications for the way in which the research topic has been interpreted. If we examine the children's referral to special schools, we are concerned with the process by which children are labelled and categorised as different. We are searching for the special processes by which they are singled out, and we examine the terminology used to characterise them (Mongon and others, 1989).

When we study the way residential special schools are organised, we are looking for important indicators of the ways in which children's problems are systematically interpreted and dealt with by schools. Schools are not simply reacting to behaviour; they build up distinctive frameworks and routines that shape children's experience in powerful ways. Later, the literature on what schools can achieve for pupils will be related to the present findings (Reynolds, 1991; Reynolds and Sullivan, 1987).

Similarly, we look at accounts of the children's progress in order to find out if the relationships between school, family and child have created a basis for change. The method for assessing progress reflects this multiple network of relationships and perceptions (Parker and others, 1991). Throughout, relationships between the child and significant social institutions, such as families and schools, have been at the heart of the research.

Summary of research aims

The main aims of the study were therefore twofold:

- to examine retrospectively the process of referral of boys and girls to residential EBD schools and their reported characteristics at admission;
- to study the perceived outcomes of at least a year's schooling in a range of provision run by local authorities and other agencies.

It was not intended to conduct a national survey – a task beyond our capabilities – but to concentrate on children's careers as they passed through this sector. In particular, it was important to shed light on whether children's situations had improved, not only in terms of academic achievement, but in resolving personal or relationship difficulties and in attaining normal developmental goals.

The selection of schools

It was felt that the best sampling strategy for these purposes was, first of all, to set criteria based partly on the child population and partly on school characteristics. Thus, it was important to include girls and children from minority ethnic groups. The schools in the study also needed to reflect the various administrative statuses of EBD schools, and to be well-established. So the sample contained two local authority as well as one independent and one non-maintained schools. It was desirable to clarify the status and function of particular schools. A systematic search was, therefore, made in neighbouring regions in order to find schools with different statuses but drawing on a similar local population. This search was partly fruitful, enabling some children referred from one local authority to be studied in two different schools. But in some other areas it was not possible to pursue this approach, especially if a major upheaval in local EBD provision was pending. The question of local policy and function also led us to select one school which, run by a large urban local authority, offered the only residential provision in the locality for girls with an EBD label. These research enquiries ranged over Wales, the South and West of England and the Midlands, where the four schools eventually chosen were based.

As the field was explored, it became evident that each school seemed to possess a distinctive ethos. Much of the literature supported this notion (Dawson, 1980). Accordingly, it was decided to look more closely at school differences, although this was not a primary aim of the project and posed significant difficulties (Rutter and others, 1979). Our sampling of schools therefore included some reference to school ethos and we felt it a bonus that the eventual sample comprised: two very different examples of behavioural approaches; a school that emphasised a developmental model of personalised care; and another that drew purposefully on a range of approaches. We are not, of course, suggesting that the four schools were nationally representative, though their styles of work represent well-known alternatives. It was not intended to test rigorously the effectiveness of particular approaches – a task that would have required a different starting point. However, there were advantages in drawing the sample widely enough to take some account of familiar differences in approach. These are explored in the chapter on children's progress as well as the chapter on systems and practices. A brief summary at this stage will, it is hoped, suffice.

Summary profile of the schools

There was a distinctive approach in each school, which can be profiled as follows:

School 1: A **system** model was adopted, emphasising a balance of strategies, including externally certified examinations, the development of good relationships, the use of rewards, and a detailed prescription of basic care tasks. Such a systematic attempt to address consistently a range of changing demands and expectations highlighted the managerial function rather than a definable philosophical commitment.

School 2: A model of **personalised group care** had been constructed.

Here the personal and individual needs of children were emphasised. Control was considered important but applied flexibly. The living units were carefully separated and differentiated to suit children's assessed needs. The school was organised mainly through a primary-style curriculum in which the personal relationships with class teachers were a significant feature. A developmental psychology provided this model with its conceptual underpinning.

School 3: A model of **encouraged achievements** pervaded both the care and educational dimensions. Behavioural principles had influenced the development of a system of school awards for the achievement of personal targets. The prevalence of learning difficulties was acknowledged by giving extra time and attention to basic educational skills, and by introducing substantial resources of information technology. It was not surprising, therefore, that a school manufacturing enterprise figured as an intended focus of pride and achievement.

School 4: Behavioural principles were also a powerful point of reference but here the model was of **disciplined achievement**. A differentiated and hierarchical house system had been devised to change behaviour by rewarding compliance and achievement and penalising misbehaviour. A full-scale and highly detailed 'token economy', covering both care and education, provided a basic structure in the lower house units. Further, more refined, behavioural strategies were used in other houses. Standard criteria were applied to govern the promotion and demotion of children from house to house, each of which represented a clear progression in material conditions and freedom. Organised group sessions were held daily, following, to various degrees, the principles of 'positive peer culture' which was the main strategy in the highest house (Vorrath and Brendtro, 1985). Punctuality, order and supervision were important baselines for practice. A secondary school curriculum aiming at GCSE was followed. A behavioural philosophy was therefore central, though peer influences were also purposefully addressed.

Thus, the schools were selected to represent a range of statuses, geographical areas and methods of work. It was not, however, possible to test particular theories about the causes or treatment of behaviour difficulties, since standardised samples of children and forms of intervention were not obtainable. Instead it was intended to learn more about the normal range of referrals and the variety of approaches which have been applied in practice. It was hoped that the resulting study of outcomes would produce realistic, if not definitive, conclusions about what followed from referral onwards.

Ethical and methodological considerations

Discussion with schools led to a careful reconsideration of the boundaries of research confidentiality. While researchers normally offer their subjects a promise of confidentiality, it was felt by schools that there should be limits to the scope of research confidentiality in the particular case of vulnerable children who might report experiences of abuse. Accordingly, after discussion with colleagues at the National Children's Bureau, guidelines were drafted to define those serious cases of alleged abuse where absolute research confidentiality would not be applicable. It was always explained to children at the outset that confidentiality would not apply in these exceptional circumstances. Our orientation was based on the child protection guidance associated with the Children Act 1989. In addition, those involved in the research were given police checks for relevant convictions.

In many ways this negotiation was a salutary introduction to the world of EBD in the 1990s. Not only was there a cloud of suspicion hanging over the residential sector in the light of Castle Hill and Pindown, there was equally a very professional awareness among schools about the kind of experiences undergone by their children which were later to be confirmed by the research. Negotiations on confidentiality were, therefore, a foretaste of the complications and anxieties within the contemporary EBD sector.

Once the four schools had been identified, the next task was to identify a sample of children who had been resident for at least a year. Ideally we were seeking 20 children in each school. The residence criterion reduced the size of the relevant sample in each school by as much as two thirds in one case. The ebbs and flows of referral and departure needed to be carefully taken into account. Because of the prevalence of learning difficulties in one school, cases were carefully screened to ensure that behaviour difficulties were also involved. Permission was sought from the parents and from all the referring local authorities to approach the child and to examine case documents. Only in one case did a parent object. Children were given a personal letter of introduction which proved so acceptable that some children not in the sample had to be reassured about the reasons for not receiving one!

Inclusion in the eventual sample depended on whether the individual child interview could be obtained. Those who ceased attending during the study period, apart from early leavers, were therefore excluded from consideration. Because interviews took place towards the end of the school year, one difficulty in three schools was posed by early leaving: four out of 15 early leavers in all were lost to the study, the highest loss being two out of three in one school. One of these also refused an interview. Unfortunately three further possible sample replacements had also left early.

Another problem was caused by temporary commitments or contingencies, which caused the loss of three cases. One child was eventually tracked down to a secure unit in another county and successfully interviewed! Only two children in all refused to be interviewed.

The following table represents the proportion of successfully achieved cases from among the available target sample, showing the rate of success to be 88 per cent.

Table 1.4 Cases successfully included in the study

	School 1	School 2	School 3	School 4	All
Cases in the study	17	14	18	18	67
Cases lost	2	4	3	0	9

A significant amount of time was spent in each school during 1992, amounting in all to some 76 days, about two thirds of which were overnight stays. Within each, classes were systematically observed and some out-of-school activities were followed. Information about the curriculum and daily living was gathered during these visits and a long interview with each head took place. This forms the basis for the chapter on system and practice. The referral documents of each child were also studied and the results are reported in the next chapter. Semi-structured interviews were arranged with small groups of children, as a preliminary to the multiple assessments of progress. Though productive, they were seen as methodologically distinct and it is hoped to report them separately.

In the major assessment, described in the chapter on progress (chapter 5), a personal questionnaire schedule was used to elicit the child's perspective on the past year; a set of assessment schedules about each individual was completed by up to four teaching and care staff; and parents were also sent a brief postal questionnaire. Using various sources, it was hoped that the broad population and structure of the school would be clarified so that the detailed multiple assessments of progress might be better understood.

Residential provision occupies a particular space in our imagination because it seems to offer an alternative to many people's experience of childhood. Yet the task it sets itself is to prepare children for their return to the world most of us inhabit. For the disadvantaged, that world is often, in fact, a harsher version than the one many of us encounter, demanding the skills to survive in an environment where homes and jobs are at a premium (Garnett, 1992). Can schools devise successful programmes that confront children's difficulties at referral and shape their potential for this unwelcoming future? This is the central question for policy and practice, which the present study begins to address.

A note on statistical analysis

The analysis of findings largely used non-parametric tests – Kruskal-Wallis and Mann-Whitney. These do not depend on assumptions about the distribution of samples. Where p is shown in the text as <.01 or <.05, this relates to findings of at least the .01 or .05 levels of significance. The smaller the quoted percentage, the greater is the degree of statistical significance.

Alternatively, where the Pearson correlation coefficient is used, this is shown as r.

2. Children's referral and their reported characteristics at admission

This chapter looks closely at the referral documents for the sample of 67 children admitted to the four schools. It seeks to clarify aspects of the formal statementing of special educational need required by law and to discuss other administrative arrangements concerning placement. It also describes the family circumstances of the children and the prevalence of substitute care experiences. The reports are then used to present a description of the social and educational problems recorded at the time of referral and prior to admission.

It is not intended to produce a definitive picture of the children but to show them and their circumstances as they appeared to the people involved in referral. These include the labels that were considered by professionals and administrators to make a convincing case for referral to a residential special school for children with EBD. Another important topic is children's schooling history. Did they come straight from mainstream schools or were their experiences more complex? How many were recorded as having learning difficulties? As a whole, the profiles of characteristics discussed in this chapter resembled curriculum vitae that gave children entry to the residential EBD school sector. They also formed the starting point for the services and interventions of the schools.

The children in the sample

Table 2.1   Age at admission by school

	Age	8	9	10	11	12	13	14	15	All
School 1		0	0	1	5	4	3	4	0	17
2		0	1	0	3	5	1	2	2	14
3		1	0	0	7	6	3	1	0	18
4		0	0	1	0	1	8	7	1	18
Total		1	1	2	15	16	15	14	3	67

The general distribution of cases showed a clear pattern, with most admissions at ages between 11 and 14. The most frequent age at admission was 12 years of age. But there were differences between schools, with School 4, in particular, having a markedly older intake. In each school, we found one child admitted under the age of 11, while two of the schools admitted 15-year-olds. If such variations are widespread they imply a rather more complex task for schools than might be assumed (HMI, 1989).

Table 2.2   Gender by school

		Male	Female	Total
School	1	6	11	17
	2	12	2	14
	3	13	5	18
	4	14	4	18
Total		45	22	67

Unusually, School 1 showed a preponderance of girls. Elsewhere, the male – female ratio followed the more typical pattern, with boys outnumbering girls (HMI, 1989; Cooper and others, 1991).

Table 2.3   Ethnicity by school

		White	African-Caribbean	Indian	Mixed parentage
School	1	14	1	0	2
	2	13	1	0	0
	3	15	1	1	1
	4	17	1	0	0
Total		59	4	1	3

In each school, the sample contained some children from minority ethnic groups. As in studies of the population looked after by local authorities, children of mixed parentage and those from African-Caribbean background were the leading subgroups of children from minority ethnic groups (Rowe and others, 1989).

Arrangements for admission

How children's admissions were processed is obviously important. We need to know more about the formal determination of special educational needs, especially the statementing process. Several question marks have been raised about these procedures (Malek and Kerslake, 1989; Goacher and others, 1987). The documents available in the schools did not necessarily represent the actual process in detail, which was, for our purpose, unfortunate. However, the documentary evidence gave important indications about the recorded process.

For example, children's files revealed virtually no evidence of parental involvement in formal conferences about the statementing. In a small minority of cases there was an indication of parents making comments or giving formal agreement. Parental participation has been acknowledged to have been generally problematic (House of Commons, 1987). Nor was the formal participation of children reported. However, in a proportion of cases, pre-admission visits to the school by parents and children were mentioned. Evidence about parental perspectives at this stage was gleaned from a survey to which 41 parents responded (an encouraging 61 per cent of cases). Only 40 per cent had found the LEA helpful. If more help had been offered at that time, 51 per cent would have been likely to have preferred a local day school. Indeed 58 per cent felt that more help from teachers would have contributed to maintaining the children in their previous schools. There were clearly mixed views about the appropriateness of a referral to residential special education.

The justification for **special** as distinct from mainstream education is a key concern of the 1981 Act but the statements were rarely rigorous on this point. Statements were not usually based on satisfying explicitly the formal criteria for special education laid out in the 1981 Act: in particular, whether or not parents favoured a special school; the impact on other children of proposed arrangements; and the lack of an efficient alternative to special education. However, it was common to refer to one such criterion – the lack of 'appropriate resources', other than in special schools – to meet a child's needs. This is an interesting comment in itself on both the resources and priorities of LEA decision-making, suggesting that difficulties in making adequate provision in mainstream schools were at the forefront of people's minds.

Since the children were admitted to special educational provision, it would have been expected that they might have received statements of special educational need (SEN) under the 1981 Education Act. In fact, their exact status was often complicated, in part by the existence of previous statements, in part by the practice of making 'provisional placements'.

Table 2.4   Distribution of SEN statements by school

School	1	2	3	4	Total
Specific statement	11	6	2	14	33
Relevant statement	8	5	10	5	29
Any statement	16	11	12	17	56

It is important to find out how far children's statements were up to date. The table distinguishes specific statements (those relating to the actual admission) from relevant statements (which may have been produced in the past). A few children had both types of statement. Gender appeared to make no difference to whether or not a child had a statement. Only half the sample had a statement specifically relating to the admission. Indeed, nearly a third of children had been given a provisional placement, without a specific statement. Over one sixth of the children had no statement of any kind even after at least a year in school.

Data on the time taken to complete statements adds another dimension to the interpretation. For some while, the recommended time for completion of a statement has been six months (DES, 1989). But there was a substantial variation among the sample as a whole and within schools (though data was lacking for School 2). Out of 28 statements for which data was available, 13 took at least 10 months to complete and four required over 20 months. Such findings are consistent with the variations reported in a recent national survey (HMI/Audit Commission, 1992a).

Table 2.5   Advice attached to statements

	Cases	% of sample
Educational psychologist	60	90
School	58	87
Health	50	75
Social services	22	33
Psychiatrist	14	21
Others	9	13

The most prolific providers of reports were educational psychologists and schools, followed by health services. In only about a third of the cases were social services reports made despite the fact that virtually half the sample had some contact with social services at this point. Psychiatric reports were produced in about a fifth of cases. Through looking at the reports it was possible to estimate the number of services involved with a case at admission, including specialist services such as Child Guidance.

Table 2.6   Number of services involved with children at admission (by school)

School	1	2	3	4	Total
Mean	2.18	1.71	3.28	2.06	2.33
Std. Dev.	1.05	1.27	1.02	0.87	1.99

Nearly all (94 per cent) were in contact with at least one specialist service, while the average child was in contact with over two, and two children were involved with no fewer than five services.

In each school, there was on average more than one service involved at admission, but there were variations among schools, with School 3 children in contact with over three services.

The involvement of children with services at admission indicates how their referral is shaped. More girls than boys (six girls; five boys) were in contact with Child Guidance at admission. Girls were also substantially represented among children in contact with Child and Adolescent Psychological Services (seven girls; ten boys). There were two girls involved with special medical services compared with one boy. This may point to some tendency to 'psychologise' and 'medicalise' the problems associated with girls. More information on children's **initial** contact with such services will be given in a later section.

There was a clear difference between the LEA sector and the other schools in the proportion of children originating from the local LEA. A majority of children in the independent and non-maintained sector came from outside the local LEA, while only one child in the LEA schools sample originated from outside his or her area.

Table 2.7   The distribution of children according to the LEAs from which they originated

School	1	2	3	4
From local LEA	1	5	17	18
From outside local LEA	16	9	1	0
Total	17	14	18	18

In Schools 2 and 4 the placement was usually on a 52-week basis. At School 1, placement was termly. Only in School 3 were the placements weekly, meaning that children would routinely be expected to go home at weekends and during holidays. These different arrangements influence the children's frequency of contact with their families – a topic investigated in the later chapter on outcomes. They also have some implications for the broader capacity of schools to provide children with extended services in a residential context.

Children at the schools were usually educated at the expense of the LEA. Only in Schools 1 and 2 were social services involved in direct payment. School 2, in particular, had a major financial relationship with social services. The issue of financial responsibility was clearly more important for schools outside the LEA sector. Enquiries about arrangements for children in care in the LEA schools suggested that the allocation of financial responsibility between departments for these children was not of major concern to the local authority agencies. It would be dismaying if financial arrangements were to affect the promptness or extent of placement. During the study there was evidence in one particular case of a concern with cost, expressed by a social services department, that might have brought the placement to an end. More information about financial arrangements would therefore be welcome.

This section has shown a number of underlying complications surrounding the administrative status and processes that governed children's admission. For the significant number without statements, there was a doubt about their formal status in special education. For many, there had been a chain of contacts with services and agencies which claimed various responsibilities. For several, delays in procedures added to the complexity. Even the term 'residential placement' had no uniform meaning. We shall now look at the issues which brought them to this complicated sector of the educational system.

It has not been easy to identify official criteria for a specifically residential special school placement. The Warnock Report cited a number of circumstances in which boarding might meet the need for 'a coordinated approach to a child's learning and living'. So, for example, a child with severe or complex disabilities requiring a large input of medical and other resources would qualify, as would a child needing consistent and continuous educational influence for various reasons, including having a severe emotional or behavioural disorder. Boarding was also necessary where a family could not cope with a child's severe disability or where poor social conditions or disturbed family relationships added to the child's educational difficulty (DES, 1978). Such a list of circumstances is broad enough to encompass a variety of reasons for admission. Yet its official standing has been by no means clear-cut. In order to ascertain the relevance of such themes to decisions about the actual cases in the sample, it was necessary to examine a wide range of topics in as concrete a fashion as possible.

Children's families and their homes

We have already seen that social services had a financial responsibility in a minority of the cases. At admission 32 per cent of the sample were in 'local authority care', similar to being looked after by local authority social services departments, under the Children Act 1989. The school samples differed in the proportions of children in local authority care. They formed a substantial majority in School 2 while elsewhere the position was reversed. A proportion ranging from 72 per cent in School 4 to 83 per cent in School 3 were **not** in care, compared with only 14 per cent in School 2.

Most of the children in care at School 2 were in what used to be termed 'voluntary care', the equivalent of 'accommodation' under the Children Act 1989. It would seem, therefore, that the school placement often had the function of establishing a holding position prior to any deeper involvement with social services. The proportion of the whole sample in contact with social services at admission (not necessarily 'in care') was nonetheless a good deal higher – virtually half the sample. Thus, many children were in touch with the care system but less often deeply lodged inside it. From this point of view, it is perhaps surprising that social services did not play a more prominent role in admission, for example, by providing a greater number of reports as part of the statementing process.

There were some indications that children's home conditions at admission differed significantly. The proportion living with natural or step-parents, adoptive parents or other relatives was much higher in some schools than others. In Schools 1 and 4 three-quarters of the children were residing with parents or relatives. In School 3 the proportion declined to 61 per cent and in School 2 to only 21 per cent. This is consistent with School 2's high proportion of social services cases.

The considerable number of children living at home in Schools 1 and 4 included four adopted children. Though not a large percentage, it should be a matter of great interest for those reviewing adoption policy that some children receive a substantial service not through social services but through the LEA.

The proportion of children found at admission to be on the official child protection register of their locality was not high. It ranged from one child in School 4 to two children in School 2, another small indication of the adversity experienced by children at the latter school. It would appear that, in general, when the children entered the school, families were usually not at a point of extreme crisis requiring close surveillance by all the professionals involved.

Table 2.8   Children's experience of care (by school)

School	1	2	3	4	Total
Never in care (or not recorded)	14	1	14	12	41
In care for less than a year	1	5	2	4	12
In care for more than a year	2	8	2	2	14
Total	17	14	18	18	67

Children's status at admission needs to be seen in the context of their previous experience. Table 2.8 shows that 61 per cent of the sample had never been in care and only 21 per cent had experience of being in care for more than a year. A majority had not suffered the breakdown of parenting associated with being in local authority care. Almost all admissions to School 2 had experience of care, but this was true of only a minority elsewhere. A more detailed comparison reveals that School 4, for example, had a number of children with less than one year's experience of care but the sample in School 2 mostly had more than a year's experience. The analysis by gender showed an even pattern, although girls were more frequent in the longer term care group than in the short term group. There was also only one girl in 'voluntary care' compared with eight boys. In general, the findings show that residential special education and local authority care were separate and distinct channels for children with emotional and behavioural difficulties, though for a minority there was a very clear overlap. A similar conclusion is apparent from the recent findings of Gemal (1993). The overlap appears much more evident among the 'therapeutic community' establishments (Beedell, 1993).

The pattern of ethnic representation was not open to straightforward interpretation because of the low number of children from minority ethnic groups. But there was a higher proportion of black and Asian children with experience of care than of white children (four out of eight, compared with 22 out of 58). However, it seemed that being in care was for black children not a stimulus to referral as they were less frequently in care during the year prior to admission.

Experiences of care in the last year again showed School 2 in the lead with 8 cases and School 4 following behind with 7 cases. There was no difference between girls and boys in this respect. The high frequency of children in care at School 2 was reinforced by the fact that four had no home base.

The proportion of girls living at home with their parents was slightly higher than their number would have suggested. The same was true of those children who had married parents. In the light of girls' presence in the longer term care group, these findings indicate very tentatively that the home situations of girls were more diverse than those of boys.

Family problems and relationships

It is now possible to begin describing the characteristics attributed to families by those preparing reports about the cases. These were noted in terms of the classifications listed below:

Table 2.9   Family problems recorded at admission

	Cases	% of sample
Up to 25% of cases		
Reconstituted family/membership changes	14	21
History of inadequate inconsistent control	13	19
History of physical abuse to child/young person	10	15
History of marital violence	8	12
Up to 10% of cases		
Physical handicap/disability of member	7	10
History of neglect/other children	7	10
Relationship problems with spouse/partner	6	9
History of sexual abuse to child/young person	6	9
Poor housing/inadequate conditions	6	9
Severe financial difficulties	6	9
History of inadequate inconsistent care	6	9
Divorce/other anomalous situations	5	7
History of neglect to child/young person	5	7
History of emotional abuse to child/young person	4	6

	Cases	% of sample
Up to 5% of cases		
History of physical abuse to other children	3	4
Homelessness/threat of eviction	3	4
Migration	3	4
Physical ill-health of member	2	3
Mental ill-health/disturbance of member	2	3
Alcohol dependence of member	2	3
Prostitution of member	2	3
History of emotional abuse to other children	2	3
History of sexual abuse to other children	2	3
History of relationship problems with child	2	3
Death of member	1	1
Mental handicap of member	1	1
Drug dependence of member	1	1
Hospitalisation of member	1	1
Imprisonment of member	1	1
No local family network available	1	1
Stress or disturbances at work	1	1
Other problems	2	3

The recorded family problems reflected various areas of difficulty, the most frequent indicating patterns of abuse and conflict within a reconstituted family situation. Other themes concerned the impact of material privation and disadvantage, as well as issues of health and disability. The average number of family problems was two, but there was a wide range from zero to eight. A large majority (79 per cent) were recorded as having at least one family problem.

There was no strong evidence that the distribution of family problem areas differed markedly among schools. Children at School 1 had the highest frequency of problems associated with family membership changes (six cases) but no cases of marital violence, physical handicap, sexual abuse to the child, poor housing or severe financial difficulties were recorded there. Those at School 2 had the highest frequency of previous inadequate control (six cases) but no recorded cases of difficulties associated with divorce or other anomalous family situations. Children at School 3 had the highest frequency of physical disability at home (five cases) but no recorded instances of previous inadequate care. Those at School 4 had the highest frequency of previous physical abuse (four) and here there were no instances of unclassified problems.

The distribution of the most frequent family problem types was not evidently related to gender or ethnicity. For example, there were ten boys and four girls who were reported as having difficulties relating to the reconstitution of families. These were divided into 11 white and two black and Asian children.

Table 2.10   Relationship problems at home recorded at admission

	Cases	% of sample
Control problems at home	42	63
Relationship between child and other children	12	18
Stealing from home	11	16
Destructive behaviour towards home	10	15
History of running away from home	8	12
Rejection of child	7	10
Relationship problems between adult and child	7	10
Neglect of child	3	4
Emotional abuse of child	2	3
Overprotection of child	2	3
Indifferent to child	1	1
Sexual abuse of child	1	1
Other problems	1	1

Control at home clearly presented the most frequently recorded domestic problem. Indeed, on a further summary measure of problems, non-compliance at home was found in 73 per cent of cases. Instances of difficult behaviour at home were rather less frequently specified. It was not common for relationships to be analysed in terms sufficiently specific to 'diagnose' family relationships. As we shall see again, the problems manifested by the child were more likely to be identified than the relationships in which they occurred.

Control issues at home were most frequently identified in cases at School 3 as were problems in relationships with other children and destructive behaviour. Stealing from home was most frequently reported in cases at School 4, and running away at School 2 (although these differences are very small). School 2 was also the marginal leader in reports of a child being rejected. There were no unusual features in the gender distribution of control issues. The ethnic distribution of control issues showed a very slightly higher percentage of difficulties among minority ethnic group children than would have been expected. Children from these groups were, therefore, not readily distinguishable from others on the criterion of domestic problems of control – a point made by previous research (Rutter and others, 1974). Problems with other children at home had the same frequency among girls as boys, despite the substantially higher representation of boys in the sample. Stealing from home was reported only of white children.

Children's behaviour and problems

This section examines the incidence of general disturbing behaviour, deficient social skills, and emotional or personal problems from the perspective of people involved in referral.

Table 2.11   Disturbing behaviour recorded at admission

	Cases	% of sample
Disruptive behaviour	33	49
Physical aggression to children	32	48
Verbal abuse	28	42
Temper tantrums	20	30
Attention-seeking	20	30
Offending	14	21
Ignoring instructions	11	16
Physical aggression to adults	10	15
Lying	10	15
Inappropriate sexual behaviour	10	15
Manipulativeness	8	12
Firelighting	5	7
Hyperactive behaviour	5	7
Self-injury	2	3
Sexual offence/abuse	1	1
Other problems	4	6

The most frequent instances of disturbing behaviour were forms of aggression and disruption rather than offending. These are also types of behaviour that are more likely to come to adult attention or to be reported by other children. However, it is also clear that strictly juvenile justice concerns did not figure predominantly. Earlier research showed that disorders of conduct, as they are called, characterised a substantial proportion of children in the 'maladjusted' special schools (Wilson and Evans, 1980).

Disruptiveness was most frequently a characteristic of children at School 4, followed by School 1. Admissions to School 4 were also most frequently depicted as aggressive to other children – a description applied to males in disproportionate numbers. In addition School 4 led in the number of children described as abusive. Children with temper tantrums were more evenly distributed, with School 3 taking a small lead. Girls were almost as numerous as boys in this category. Attention-seeking followed a similar pattern, with School 1 pre-eminent. Offending, on the other hand, was most common among admissions to Schools 2 and 4, and among boys. Aggression directed at adults was also more frequent among the intake of those schools.

Inappropriate sexual behaviour was said to be most frequent among the group in School 2 but was absent from those at School 4. It was a description applied to the behaviour of more girls than boys. It is important to note the extent to which girls' misbehaviour is seen in sexual terms (Lees, 1989). Lying was reported most frequently, by a small margin, among the intake of School 4 and among boys. However, manipulativeness was portrayed most often among those at School 2. Firelighting was also described most frequently at School 2 and confined to boys.

Hyperactivity, on the other hand, was clearly most frequently reported among admissions to School 3. Self-injury was confined to children admitted to School 4. In addition one male at School 2 was alleged to have perpetrated sexual abuse.

Five children with recorded offences were admitted, located at Schools 1 and 4. They made up seven per cent of the sample. The highest number of offences was three, committed by a boy at School 4. In four cases (six per cent of the sample), offences had been recorded in the previous year, suggesting that offending had possibly played a part in the referral of at least some children.

Table 2.12   Social skills difficulties recorded at admission

	Cases	% of sample
Poor relationships with peers	44	66
Socially isolated	10	15
Poor relationships with adults	8	12
Poor presentation/social skills	5	7
Problems relating to opposite sex	2	3
No sustaining interests/hobbies	2	3

'Poor relationships with peers' were described in a majority of cases. Such a generalised description is not very informative but it does appear to mark out a major area of concern for adults in the statementing process. Social (rather than cultural) isolation was the next most frequent problem, followed by some general difficulty with adults. Peer relationships were most frequently problematic among children admitted to School 1, followed by those at Schools 2 and 3. Social isolation was also most frequent at School 1, and applied more often to girls than boys.

Table 2.13   Emotional and personal problems assessed at admission

	Cases	% of sample
Poor self-concept	21	31
Immature or precocious	6	9
Anxious	6	9
Egocentric	3	4
Depressive	3	4
Extreme introversion	1	1
Fears or phobias	1	1
Other problems	5	7

By far the most common description of an emotional and personal problem was of poor self-concept, followed by much less frequent problems of maturity and anxiety. Self-concept problems were most common in School 1 and least common in School 4. Boys outnumbered girls in this category, but only by a ratio of four to three. Each of the four children stated in the documentation to be African-Caribbean was also regarded by having a poor self-concept, compared with 17 of the 59 children stated to be white. Similarly, seven of those 16 children who in the research interviews classified themselves as black or Asian, or were uncertain of their ethnic identity, fell into this category, compared with fourteen of the 49 children who classified themselves as white. However, no children were said at admission to be uncertain of their ethnic identity. Given the frequent appearance of self-concept in reports, its application to cases, especially to African-Caribbean children, requires more investigation. Turning now to other problems, it was found that School 1 also had the highest number of admissions with anxiety and with problems of maturity. Girls again were strongly represented in both these categories. Depression was reported only in Schools 1 and 3, and only among white children. Egocentricity characterised males only and was found in Schools 1 and 4. Most of the descriptions of miscellaneous difficulties were applied to children admitted to School 3. In general, 46 per cent of children were described as having at least one emotional problem.

The descriptions of emotional and personal problems were therefore much less frequent than the descriptions of control and behavioural problems. The children's problems were generally defined in terms of disruption rather than inner crisis. The process of referral was concentrated upon pragmatic concerns rather than profound diagnosis.

Health assessment

The health of children showing behaviour difficulties or entering substitute care is known to be a subject of concern (Rutter, 1975; Bamford and Wolkind, 1988). How was the health of these children assessed in practice?

In 64 per cent of cases there was evidence of a medical examination around the time of admission. The proportions of boys and girls described as healthy at admission were roughly similar – 66 per cent of boys compared with 59 per cent of girls. Children's health history, however, should not be overlooked. For example, 27 per cent of children had at some time undergone a serious illness, 31 per cent requiring hospitalisation. Seven per cent had been ill in the previous year. Less crucially perhaps, but nonetheless important for schools, four per cent of the sample did not wear the spectacles prescribed for them.

Table 2.14 Physical and medical problems at admission

	Cases	% of sample
Enuresis	11	16
Poor hygiene	6	9
Defective hearing/vision/speech	6	9
Encopresis	6	9
Eating disorder	4	6
Epilepsy	4	6
Other chronic condition	4	6
Unspecified drug abuse	3	4
Asthma	2	3
Prescribed drug misuse	1	1
Excessive smoking	1	1
Poor physical condition	1	1
Brain damage	1	1
Eczema	1	1
Other problems	3	4

The most frequent physical and medical problems were related to hygiene. However, enuresis, in particular, has been found to be associated with emotional and behavioural difficulties (Rutter, 1975). Problems of communication featured rather less prominently, as did neurological difficulties. The general rate of behaviourally-related difficulties such as drug abuse was comparatively low. School 1 had no children with epilepsy, while School 2 had no children with communication difficulties, but the highest number with encopresis (four). School 3 had the most children with enuresis (five). The only child with brain damage was found in School 4.

Girls outnumbered boys in having communication difficulties, epilepsy, eating disorders, engaging in unspecific drug abuse and in other miscellaneous problems. Children with asthma consisted of two girls; one girl had eczema, while a girl was responsible for the one case of prescribed drug misuse. One boy was described as smoking excessively and one was said to be in poor physical condition. These apparently small numbers of specific physical and medical problems emphasise nonetheless the demands of caring for individual needs in a form of educational provision that is not a specialist health facility.

A list of possible impairments was also used to collect more specific data on children's health difficulties. This showed that 27 per cent had at least one health impairment – a substantial proportion. These results have also been used to calculate mean scores which were then included alongside other scores in Table 2.16. That table presents averages for all the problem areas identified. Before examining this data, however, we need to look at the final but clearly crucial problem area – educational behaviour.

Educational behaviour

It was not wholly surprising that problems of educational behaviour featured frequently in reports at admission.

Table 2.15   Educational behaviour assessed at admission

	Cases	% of sample
Behaviour problem	57	85
Making trouble in class	48	72
Poor concentration	36	54
Attendance	19	28
Performance	15	22
Exclusion	13	19
Other problem	1	1

The most widespread problem lay in the general category of unacceptable behaviour, such as disrupting lessons or ignoring instructions. Poor concentration was also frequent. Some of the specific issues affected less than a third of the sample. Problems of performance were identified in cases where children appeared not to be working to their ability. Attendance difficulties were more frequent than problems of exclusion. Unacceptable behaviour was universally recorded in School 4's cases but slightly diminished elsewhere, reaching a low of 65 per cent in School 1. It was found that boys outweighed girls in this category more than their numbers would have suggested. Minority ethnic groups were, if anything, slightly under-represented in the main category of unacceptable behaviour. Attendance problems and underperformance were most concentrated in School 4 but by a very small margin. Only white children were reported as having problems of attendance. Exclusion was recorded most often in

Schools 1 and 4. In general, it is clear that the children were most frequently labelled as disruptive and the findings tend to suggest that this was a major factor in referral.

Children's problems summarised

While the data so far indicates something about the distribution of problems among categories in the sample, it is also necessary to look at the accumulated weight of problems attributed to individuals. For this purpose, they were added to create scores in the general problem areas. These were calculated for each individual and then averaged. In order to simplify the scores for school behaviour, the **general** category of 'behaviour problem', affecting 85 per cent of the sample, was added to attendance and the items listed below it in Table 2.15. The results for each problem area are shown in the next table.

In general, the composition of children's scores reflects the various aspects of perceived difficulty. These in turn depend on various social contexts of judgement, for example, those prevailing in a particular area (HMI/Audit Commission, 1992a). Nonetheless, the average scores for the whole sample demonstrate the comparative importance of behaviour problems, in terms of both educational and more generally disturbing behaviour, in shaping the referral and assessment process. Given the numerous possible types of family problems which were listed, the average score here may appear on the low side. As the reported standard deviation indicates, there was a large range of scores on this measure, from 21 per cent with **no** recorded family problems to one child with **eight!**

The data indicated some differences among the schools, although these were not always statistically significant. On average, family problems were perceived as most acute for children at School 2 but domestic relationships were most fraught in the School 3 sample. School 2 also admitted children with the highest average rate of disturbing behaviour, closely followed by School 4. Deficits in social skills as well as emotional or personal problems were significantly more numerous at School 1 ($p<.05$ and $<.01$). School 4 received those with the greatest average rate of difficulty in educational behaviour ($p<.01$). Interestingly, these two schools shared a major source of admissions, in the form of one particular LEA; the differences in descriptions of their children perhaps suggest that they had received clientele identified as having different needs. School 2 admitted children with the highest average number of general physical problems but children at School 1 on average possessed the most impairments.

School	Family problems	Relationships at home	Disturbing behaviour	Social skills deficit	Emotional and personal	Educational behaviour	Physical problems	Impairments
1 Mean	1.29	1.59	2.65	1.53	1.35	1.47	0.94	0.47
Std. (Dev.)	1.05	1.12	1.87	0.87	1.12	0.80	1.14	0.72
2 Mean	3.00	1.50	3.79	0.86	0.42	1.36	1.00	0.36
Std. (Dev.)	2.54	1.09	1.19	0.77	0.65	0.63	1.11	0.50
3 Mean	2.17	1.94	2.83	1.17	0.67	1.33	0.72	0.28
Std. (Dev.)	1.89	0.94	1.38	1.10	0.69	0.84	1.02	0.58
4 Mean	2.00	1.44	3.56	0.67	0.28	2.06	0.61	0.17
Std. (Dev.)	2.40	1.10	0.98	0.69	0.57	0.64	0.92	0.38
All Mean	2.07	1.63	3.18	1.06	0.69	1.57	0.81	0.31
Std. (Dev.)	2.07	1.44	1.44	0.92	0.87	0.78	1.03	0.56

These data, on their own, do not allow us to be conclusive about any differences in the process by which children have been matched to schools. In other words, it is difficult to conclude whether or not children were being systematically selected for one type of school on the basis of certain characteristics, though the findings for Schools 1 and 4 are intriguing. The data do, however, tell us more about the outcome of the referral and admission process, indicating a range of characteristics which show some common problem areas but also differentiate the schools' intakes in some degree. To understand better how children have fared educationally in the past we shall now look at data about children's previous schooling.

Children's previous schooling and experience of educational services

Having examined the range and intensity of alleged problems in the behavioural field, it is now appropriate to give more concentrated attention to children's educational comptences, their educational history and the services to which they had been given access.

Basic educational skills are often found to be problematic in children with behaviour difficulties (Rutter and others, 1970; Davie and others, 1972). Whatever the causal relationships involved, it is clear that such children must be doubly disadvantaged in the school setting (Pumfrey and Reason, 1991). Data on the basic educational competences of children were gleaned from the psychologists' reports at admission. The test data shows at which normal age level the children had performed. It also indicates the variation in test use as well as in results.

Table 2.17   Performance in age-related tests of basic educational skills at admission

	Cases	Below10 years	10 year/s or above	Minimum	Maximum
Reading accuracy	11	8	3	6	11
Reading comprehension	14	12	2	6	11
General reading	31	18	13	6	13
Mathematics	16	12	4	7	14
Spelling	20	17	3	6	12

Nine different reading tests were used, most of which focused on general skills, others on comprehension or on a combination of accuracy and comprehension. Six different mathematics tests were employed by psychologists as well as five different spelling tests. The children to whom these tests related numbered 45, or 67 per cent of the sample.

The results taken as a whole indicated a substantial proportion of children with reading competences below their chronological age, even by a minimal standard of ten years. While only three per cent of the sample were aged under ten at admission, a clear majority of those tested had competences below this age. Where tests for other basic skills had been given, the picture was also discouraging. Equally the results imply that educational psychologists would have been concerned about many children's progress. Attention must therefore be paid to the services provided not only for EBD but for learning difficulties (LD).

In order to understand children's careers more fully, it is important to trace their schooling history, especially in the light of the 'integrationist' philosophy associated with the 1981 Education Act. It would be consistent with the philosophy to find that children were given access to an extensive network of services provided in mainstream schools or in temporary day provision. To what extent was this the case, first of all, in mainstream schools?

Table 2.18   Specialist services in mainstream school

	EBD		Learning Difficulties	
	No.	%	No.	%
Class teacher's programme	4	6	1	1
Specialist teacher	11	16	4	6
Therapist/counsellor	1	1	0	0
Individual supporter in classroom	4	6	1	1
Special part-time class	8	12	9	13
Special full-time class	5	7	2	3
Onsite unit	2	3	1	1
Other school service	3	4	0	0

The most frequently provided services were the use of specialist teachers and part-time classes. On-site or full-time classes were also employed. There are, however, considerable doubts about the usefulness of special classes (Coulby and Harper, 1985). Therapists and professionals giving individual classroom support were infrequent. A study has recently pointed to the unavailability of therapists (Association of Child Therapists/The Child Psychotherapy Trust, 1992). Services that work intensively on individual cases, such as behaviour support teams, have also been found to be thin on the ground (Moses and others, 1988). In all 64 per cent received at least one service of some kind while 27 per cent received one or more services for learning difficulties and 49 per cent one or more services for EBD. The services offered at this stage have important implications for children's careers.

Apart from services in school, there are also specialist services that have been accessible to children in mainstream provision. The next table describes the stages at which contact took place.

Table 2.19   First contact with specialist services

Service	Age at first contact			
	Under 5	5 to 10	11 to 15	Total
Educational psychologist	4	32	18	54
Child Guidance	2	10	7	19
Child/Adolescent Psychological Service	2	6	10	18
Speech therapy	5	7	0	12
Education welfare	0	2	5	7

The data shows that a substantial proportion of those children who did receive services were in contact with services at the pre-school and primary stage. No fewer than 54 per cent had contact with an educational psychologist before the age of 11, while 18 per cent had similarly early contacts with speech therapists and also with Child Guidance. It is clear that for many of these the question was not one of a late, surprise referral but of an early contact with services. It may be asked why specialist contact was not successful in preventing an escalation of problems – a question increasingly posed by educationalists (Reid, 1986). The effect of the services cannot, however, be straightforwardly evaluated in the present study. For some children, contact with a specialist meant referral to special education at the primary stage. But the data suggest that for a proportion of cases access to specialist services was not delayed.

Indeed, it appears that there was more frequently a contact with specialist services than with a service in mainstream school. Nearly all the children

(94 per cent) had experienced contact with a specialist service, chiefly with the educational psychologist who prepared a report (89 per cent). At some stage, there had been a contact with Child Guidance in 28 per cent of cases and with a Child/Adolescent Psychological Service in 27 per cent of cases. Specialist services may therefore have facilitated entry to the special schools sector.

From the contribution of specialist services we now turn to the children's school histories, in particular to their experience of special schools.

Table 2.20   Specialist schooling provision attended prior to admission

	Cases	% of sample
Boarding special school (EBD)	19	28
Day special school (MLD)	10	15
Day unit	9	13
Hospital school	6	9
Day special school (unclassified)	3	4
Unclassified school	3	4
Observation and Assessment Centre School	2	3
Day special school (EBD)	1	1
Boarding special school (MLD)	1	1
Boarding special school (unclassified)	1	1

In cases where day provision had been tried and failed, entry to a Day unit would be an understandable prelude to a residential admission. But only 13 per cent of the sample – a surprisingly low proportion – had gone along that route. Similarly, only one child had attended a day special school for EBD. These results suggest that day provision formed a sector very distinct from residential provision. Contrary to expectations, there appeared to be no graduated continuum of provision but instead there existed divergent sectors (Topping, 1983).

Educational difficulties were reflected in the background of the 15 per cent of children who had attended a day special school for pupils with moderate learning difficulties. This experience characterised as many girls as boys. Only one child – a girl – was found to have attended a boarding school for pupils with learning difficulties. It seemed that previous boarding experience of other kinds was a more frequent characteristic.

A previous experience of a residential EBD school characterised nearly one third of the sample – an unexpectedly high proportion. Much of this was accounted for by School 3, characterising no less than 61 per cent of that school's sample. In part, such admissions were transfers from primary residential settings. In other cases, they represented responses to problems in parallel secondary settings. There seemed little difference between the proportion of boys and girls with this experience. (To this total should be added one further girl who had been placed in an unclassified special boarding school.) Hospital schools featured in the experience of nine per cent of the sample, more especially in School 3 – a confirmation of the importance of special provision as an avenue into that school.

One measure of this complex schooling history is the number of changes of school, not due to age, which children have experienced.

Table 2.21   Changes of school not due to age

	Cases	%
None	15	22
One	23	34
Two	12	18
Three	4	6
Four	3	4
Five	2	3
Six	1	1

For ten children, the table shows three or more changes of school not due to age – a significant experience of discontinuity. The following table shows the last provision experienced by children before admission.

Table 2.22   Current schooling immediately prior to admission

	Cases	% of sample
Mainstream secondary	22	33
Special boarding school (EBD)	16	24
Unspecified provision	9	13
Mainstream primary school	8	12
Day special (MLD or SLD)	4	6
Other day special	2	3
Observation and Assessment Unit	2	3
Day special school (EBD)	1	1
Other special boarding school	1	1
Hospital school	1	1

The data suggest that many children were fed into their new schools from mainstream provision. But 46 per cent came from other special provision including other EBD schools. Intermediate provision attended on a daily basis was again not strongly in evidence. However, there is a further major group to be taken into account. There were 14 children who were considered not to be attending schools prior to admission, nine of whom (13 per cent of the sample) had been excluded. For these children who had not been attending school in the immediate past, there had been real problems of continuity in their schooling. Data was available on ten children (15 per cent of the sample) who were judged to have lost formal schooling prior to admission, ranging from one month to a year. Seven (or ten per cent of the sample) had lost over six months of schooling. These were faced with a significant hill to climb when finally admitted.

Routes into residential EBD schooling were, therefore, open both from mainstream and from special schools, as well as from the population of children without schooling. It is difficult, as we have seen, to chart a logical career which relates residential schooling to a systematic set of resources and of criteria for access to them. Despite contact with specialist services, often at an early age, children's experiences of schools and services did not show an organised pattern of preventive work. This echoes the finding of another study which suggested that, in the opinion of educational psychologists, 44 per cent of residential EBD placements could have been prevented, if certain resources had been made available (Malek and Kersdale, 1989). Thus, questions are raised about the possibly unnecessary separation of children from their homes, as well as about the efficient use of resources. We have to fall back on the previous descriptions of children, many of which echo descriptions of the 'maladjusted'. It is these that turn the key in the lock and give children access to the boarding experience.

The research suggests that a child was labelled as 'a residential EBD' case once the psychologist was satisfied that both the school and the parents were having consistent difficulties; these difficulties were often sufficient to have prompted a clinical referral. The psychologist thus acted as a screen for referrals which were prompted by concerns at school and at home; previous services had failed to solve problems. Admissions reflected, therefore, a social process by which an accumulation of visible problems was meant to be decisively addressed. It was much less straightforward to identify a clear-cut classification of underlying personal problems, even though children had come into contact with specialist services. General nonconformity of behaviour was the most common complaint. A broad conclusion is that referrals and admissions were **socially** driven rather than governed by precise considerations of clinical or educational need and treatment (Ford and others, 1982).

Summary

- The sample consisted of 67 children (45 boys and 22 girls) who had been resident for at least a year in four different coeducational schools.
- Only half of the sample had a statement specifically relating to the admission.
- About five out of six children had at some point received statements of special educational need, which often took longer than the recommended period of six months to complete.
- About a third of children were the subject of reports by social services at the time of admission but virtually half the sample were in some contact with social services at that point.
- Nine per cent were on the child protection register at admission.
- Children in non-LEA schools were frequently educated outside their home area.
- Arrangements for periods of residence differed significantly among schools.
- Financial arrangements that involved social services departments were identified in the non-LEA sector but much less frequently in the schools controlled by LEAs.
- Thirty-two per cent of children were in the care of local authorities at admission, but 61 per cent had never been in care.
- The proportion of children in care differed markedly among schools, though they were present in each. In each school there were some children with over a year's experience of local authority care.
- Children's family problems reflected various areas of reported difficulty, the most frequent relating to patterns of conflict and abuse in an unstable family situation. Material disadvantage and issues of health and disability also featured in reports. The average number of recorded family problems was two but the range lay from zero to eight.
- Controlling the child was recorded as the most frequent difficulty in domestic relationships, affecting 73 per cent of the sample.
- Aggressive and disruptive behaviour was more frequently recorded than offending. Though 21 per cent were described as having engaged in offending behaviour, only seven per cent of the sample had recorded offences. Poor relationships with peers were reported in a majority of cases.

- There was at least one emotional or personal problem in 46 per cent of cases. A poor self-concept was the most frequently recorded emotional or personal problem, affecting 31 per cent.
- Twenty-seven per cent of children had at some time undergone a serious illness. A majority were described as currently healthy but 27 per cent had at least one health impairment. The most frequently recorded physical and medical problems were related to enuresis and other issues of hygiene. Difficulties in communication and neurological problems were also significant.
- Unacceptable behaviour in school was the most common recorded difficulty in educational behaviour, affecting a very large majority of the sample (85 per cent).
- Tests in basic skills revealed a substantial proportion of children with results below their chronological age.
- Services for children when they had been in mainstream schools had included principally specialist teaching rather than individual counselling and support. However, a large proportion of children had received specialist services from sources outside school at the primary stage. Moreover, 94 per cent were receiving at least one specialist service at admission.
- Intermediate day provision had not been a common experience of the children prior to admission. Special schools in general, but especially other residential EBD schools, were substantial providers of cases to the EBD schools in the study: indeed, 46 per cent of children were admitted from other special provision. Ten per cent of children had, however, lost over six months of schooling prior to admission.
- Disconcertingly, there was evidence to suggest that children had not experienced an organised continuum of provision that might have prevented the need for referral. The behavioural difficulties they posed were more frequently described than their personal problems. The process of admission appeared, therefore, to be socially driven rather than planned according to rational criteria.

3. Systems of schooling

In this chapter we try to establish what the schools offered and, more particularly, the reasoning behind it. There have been surveys which examine what approaches are felt to benefit 'maladjusted' or 'disturbed' children (Wilson and Evans, 1980; Dawson, 1980). There is indeed a recognition of the diversity of policy and practice in residential special schools (Cole, 1986). This research has therefore sought to include that diversity by sampling schools that differed in their principles of work and in their planned resources for care and treatment. Moreover, the sampling process crossed the divide between the public sector LEA schools and the independent and non-maintained sector, as well as between smaller and larger schools.

These wider organisational differences raise questions about the management of the schools and the network of accountability surrounding them. Overshadowing those management issues, legislative changes have brought new demands. Schools were preparing to implement National Curriculum teaching and assessment. In addition the Children Act 1989 has introduced not only new arrangements for the inspection of independent boarding schools but also a substantial body of guidance that provides the impulse to create more integrated standards of care for all children in need living away from their parents. The Act arguably broadened and reinforced the emphasis on planning and review associated with the Education Act 1981. These general themes were investigated in conjunction with the more particular questions of school management.

The aim has been to combine together as a whole a study of several school features. In recent years, research has sought to identify what, as a whole, makes for an 'effective school', examining leadership, purpose, climate, expectations and teacher-pupil relations (Rutter and others, 1979; Ainscow and Muncy, 1989). We need to be especially aware of how the features of a school hang together, bearing in mind the diverse influences upon it and the changing nature of its pupil population. We begin therefore by investigating the school's management structure and ethos, before looking at questions of internal management and resources. Then the influence of some general principles – partnership with families and equal opportunities – is explored. Some key dimensions of work are examined – care, curriculum and control. Then, we try to find out more about the referral process and admission policy. Finally, we need to understand better the process by which children's school careers are planned, culminating in their departure from the school.

Accountability

'Good schools' are described as well managed (Ainscow, 1991). But what does this mean for schools that lie in different sectors with distinctive lines of accountability? In particular, how in practical terms is the ethos of the school defined? To answer these questions it was necessary to interview Heads. While Heads may possibly give a partial picture, they are best placed to present an authoritative account of what happens at the organisational interface between the school and its environment. Moreover, in examining school ethos, aspects of the school structure were studied in order to demonstrate the level of correspondence between the Head's description and the actuality. Documents on the school thus served as an additional source of evidence.

Asked to whom they were accountable, Heads mentioned a diverse group – children and parents, LEAs, governors and, in the non-LEA sector, the managers of the school. It was evident, first of all, that children and parents were not significant influences on policy. In the light of recent movements to empower 'consumers' in education, this was an important response. For local authority schools, the LEA was perceived as a source of advice rather than of policy, which one Head described as 'very thin'. Governors were regarded as part of the public relations domain, though it was important to impress them as one Head explained. Management structures in the non-LEA sector created a different line of accountability. Here, there seemed to be a tighter link which did not resemble the more discretionary structures in local authorities. For example, the Head of the independent school had daily contact with the manager to whom he was responsible.

Referring agencies were seen by one non-LEA school as making divergent demands, some with distinctly less interest than others in the progress of the child. Not surprisingly, LEA officers were generally perceived as influential brokers in the referral process. Financial questions about referral loomed largest for one non-LEA school, very much aware of the impact its financial charges made on the funding agencies. In the other non-LEA school, these contacts were left to managers, rather than the Head, but there was a similar anxiety felt by managers about a lack of money among local authorities.

Advisory structures were designed to enable the schools to draw on a range of external expertise. In the local authorities, the Heads could turn for advice to a range of specialists, including a set of curriculum advisers. In the non-LEA sector, curriculum advice tended to come from one individual expert. Significantly, links with local authority advisers were initiated by the Heads. One Head of a LEA school expressed a difficulty in knowing where to turn:

> I'm never really sure... who is in a position to advise me over any particular issue.

Only in one school, that in the non-maintained sector, were issues of 'race' and gender mentioned as part of the advisory service.

The net result of these arrangements was to place a substantial responsibility on Heads to define the school function and ethos. The centrality of the Heads' role was therefore very evident. It was not necessarily the case that they had usurped power, rather that power and responsibility were usually deemed to go together as part of the job. The means by which they sought to influence the school tended to be the management of staff. For example, one saw himself as 'an enabler of staff'. It was on the independent school that a management policy had made a significant impact. Here the Head's area of discretion was more fundamentally to do with policy implementation and with the children themselves than with making policy.

Residential special schooling for children with emotional and behavioural difficulties evidently presents a complex task. The history of such schools points to the range of treatment, education, and care that has been offered (Wilson and Evans, 1980; Laslett, 1983). More recently, it has highlighted the popularity of behavioural treatments compared with more traditional psychoanalytic concepts (Dawson, 1980). Where did the Heads stand on these fundamental issues?

School ethos

When asked about the relative importance of treatment, education, or care, the Heads were reluctant to express a distinct preference. However, some clear differences did emerge. For example, the Head of School 1 referred to the 'inextricable' link between care and education. Education was broadly conceived, encompassing the day and the evening. By the same token, the whole ambience was intended to nurture and develop children. By providing consistent role models, there was also a treatment process.

School 1 appeared therefore to adopt an eclectic position, selecting the most appropriate from different approaches. The school population was organised in a relatively undifferentiated way, without distinct units, except for a separation between girls' and boys' living accommodation. While behaviour ratings were made by staff and published for children, these were broadly grouped rather than precise. 'Class credits' could also be earned. Achieving personal targets could lead to 'treats' and praise. An emphasis on nurture coexisted with a focus on behaviour.

The Head of School 2 was committed to a philosophy of children's growth and development by stages. Education was part of the child care practice. Adopting ecological and biomedical terms, the Head said that education was for 'survival' in the community and also could be therapeutic. His pre-eminent purpose, however, appeared to be one of care.

The whole thing is child care, as far as I can see it.

Treatment was not central to his philosophy, especially behavioural treatment. The Head of School 2 opposed operant conditioning in general and identified negative aspects to a token economy for children 'acting out' a phase of behaviour. However, for some irrational behaviours, behavioural approaches were felt to be appropriate. Although acknowledging the importance of control, the Head also spoke uniquely of love and compassion, encouraging the children to value themselves. Instead of treatment, the term 'opportunity' was used.

School 2 was the most committed of all the schools to providing an appropriate caring environment for children's differently perceived needs. Thus, there were three off-site and one on-site living units when the research began. They represented the stages of growth and independence envisaged by the school's philosophy, beginning with a closely supervised nurturing unit and ending with different independence units. The school did not, however, claim to substitute for a family and could offer social work resources to help build a home base for children if one was needed.

The nurturing unit at School 2 was intended for children who had missed out this aspect of their growth and development. It facilitated regression, according to psychodynamic theory. A number of play rooms were designed to enable children, firstly to go back, and then to move forward in their development. It was set in a large house some miles from the school.

There was also a fully supervised and structured on-site unit for boys who were felt to require support and surveillance.

A further unit, located in a house away from the school site, was intended for children in their last year of schooling, emphasising a very full programme of work experience and the learning of practical 'independence' skills. A similar unit closed while the research was being undertaken. Provision at School 2 had therefore been designed to reflect a philosophy of child development.

Philosophically, the other two schools were committed to treatment, or more specifically, to the 'reduction' or 'amelioration' of problems. Both Schools 3 and 4 had adopted behavioural principles, but their versions were structurally different. At School 3 there was an emphasis on rewarding achievement, however small. Assessments were made on a daily basis of children's behaviour in relation to personal targets, in the units and in school. These assessments were brought to a weekly meeting of staff which awarded certificates to the children. A combined certificate for meeting targets in both the unit and in school represented the peak of achievement. Targets could then be reset to reflect performance. The school meeting held at the end of the week resembled a prize ceremony, with staff and children applauding one another as the paper certificates were received. It was also explained that the school offered not love but commitment and care. The pupils were housed in a relatively undifferentiated series of units, including a girls' and a mixed leavers' unit, near the school building.

The behavioural approach in School 4 put emphasis on the daily learning process by which children attend to the consequences of their behaviour, both negative and positive. An example was the 'token economy' which operated in the lower houses at all times. A behavioural perspective with clear-cut rewards and sanctions governed the disciplinary policy of the school, with token fines and loss of privileges. An accumulation of recorded achievements led the children, in theory at least, to improve their status and to progress from the lowest to the highest of the four school houses. The progressive building of a 'positive peer culture' through group praise and criticism was intended to supplement this basic approach (Vorrath and Brendtro, 1985).

School 4 was more openly committed than School 3 to the behavioural use of sanctions, or 'response costs', such as time out. Children who misbehaved seriously or persistently could also be returned to the next lowest house in the scheme and be deprived of the material privileges and comforts associated with the higher house. These privileges and comforts were carefully graduated so that each house had its position in a hierarchy of living standards. Significantly, all children admitted to the school were, without exception, allocated to the lowest house with the minimum level of comfort and were thus instructed that all privileges, such as watching television or having personal possessions, had to be earned. The contrast with School 3 was very evident.

Thought it might appear that School 4 was heavily committed to behaviourism, it was emphasised that behavioural treatment did not deal adequately with problems of self-image and other activities were necessary for this purpose. In this respect, positive peer culture draws on a different concept of group psychology, not dissimilar to mutual aid organisations such as Alcoholics Anonymous. It aims to boost self-image by the recognition that a person has helped someone else in the group. It is somewhat reminiscent of the approach followed by the 'pioneers' of special schooling in emphasising participation and responsibility though based on quite different theoretical premises (Balbernie, 1966).

Resources and management

In the next section we examine the resources available to the schools and the internal management processes. The resources include buildings and their location as well as the numbers and qualifications of staff and the availability of specialist support.

Accommodation

School 1   An adapted country house with a largely detached set of classrooms.

School 2   A set of detached residential units, one on-site, and a classroom block.

School 3   A set of detached residential units, all on-site, with a school complex.

School 4   An adapted country house with two additional on-site units and detached classrooms.

Each school had had to develop its current accommodation from a much older base unit. Nonetheless, Heads were satisfied with their buildings for the most part.

Location

School 1   Village in the countryside.
School 2   Seaside resort adjoining city.
School 3   Village in the countryside.
School 4   Bordering small town in rural area.

Though the schools were served by reasonably good communications, most were located in the countryside. Transport to and from home was a major enterprise, especially for Schools 1, 2 and 3. Each of these took pupils from beyond the county where it was located. Mini-vans and taxis were pressed into service at School 1 and School 3, requiring almost military organisation at key times, while School 2 also had to transport children daily to and from dispersed living units. Travel between school and the family home occupied several hours for the most distantly located children. Placement of children outside their local community was therefore a significant cost, both for children and schools; it also appeared questionable according to the principles of the Children Act 1989. The extent to which the Act had been taken into account in considering these placements remained unclear.

The general environment is recognised to have an effect on children's sense of well-being (Wilson and Evans, 1980). Buildings were regarded as unsatisfactory only in School 3, where redecoration of the units was considered long overdue and the over-sized classrooms needed modification and better furnishings. A school-based enterprise and young people's own work on the site were essential to compensate for a low capitation grant. Not surprisingly, local management of special schools was not an unwelcome prospect for this school. Unlike School 3, where science and information technology were well catered for, School 1 was looking to improve its science base by buying science teaching from a local college.

Table 3.1   Staff resources in the four schools

	School 1	School 2	School 3	School 4
Head	1	1	1	1
Deputy (Education)	1[x]	1	1	2
Deputy (Child Care)	2[*]	1	1	1
Senior teacher	1	–	1	1
Senior care post	–	1	–	–
Administrator	–	1	1	1
School nurse	–	–	1	1
Care team leaders	2	4	7	4
Child care workers	9	20	10	14
Additional care staff	–	–	–	4.5[0]
Teachers	4	4	8	6
Classroom assistants	2	1	1	1
Administrative staff	1	2	2	2.25
Support workers	8	9	20	17
Places for children	42	25	100	60
Occupants	29	25	64	49

[x] Unfilled
[*] 1 joint teacher/Head of Care
[0] 'Night Supervisors' – a separate function at School 4

School 2 was unhappy about its library while facilities for Craft Design and Technology were due to be upgraded. A lack of adequate maintenance was the subject of dissatisfaction at School 1, together with insufficient clerical resources. School 3 was also dissatisfied with its clerical resources and School 4 echoed a concern with maintenance.

Staff resources raised questions not simply about numbers but about qualifications and experience. The standard composition of the staff group included senior staff, teachers, classroom assistants, child care workers and support workers fulfilling basic care, administrative and maintenance functions.

Despite the fact that the schools were coeducational, the composition of the senior staff groups was predominantly male. Of 14 senior staff, only four were female and in two schools there were all-male senior staff groups. School 1 had a female care team for girls and a male team for boys. In School 2, teams were mixed, while School 3's girls' unit also had a female team. There was a preference at School 4 for employing female care staff generally. Male staff here were always accompanied in the presence of girls. The rationale for this arrangement was not so much the possible fear of endangering or threatening girls as of guarding against allegations against male staff. The possibility that boys might make allegations or that female staff might need support did not seem to weigh so heavily. However, the wider employment of female staff in these schools as a means of reducing dangers to children certainly deserves more thought.

High staffing ratios have been recommended for residential special education, with a **minimum** of one teacher for seven pupils recommended by the Warnock Committee (see also HMI, 1989). The Head of School 1 was satisfied with a ratio of one to 6.5 pupils, while there were no complaints at School 2 about a ratio of 1 to 4.5.

School 2 was, however, unable to employ classroom assistants and instead used Employment Trainees, who were not regarded as reliable. School 3 was felt to be significantly under-resourced, by two teachers and as many as ten classroom assistants. Classroom assistants varied sharply in background: in contrast to School 2, School 1 and School 4 employed graduates. The lack of training for this work has recently been confirmed in an official report (HMI, 1992).

The minimum qualification for teachers was a Teaching Certificate, though specialist qualifications were naturally welcome and at School 2 help in attending such courses would be available.

Table 3.2   Teaching staff and qualifications

	School 1	School 2	School 3	School 4
Teachers	7	6	10	10
PGCE	3	2	1	2
B. Ed	2	1	0	1
Cert. Ed	2	2	9	7
Dip. Special Ed	1	2	0	1
Post graduate				
Degree in education	1	0	3	1
Advanced diploma in Ed	4	0	0	0
Other post graduate degree	0	1	0	2

Unlike others, School 3 had no teachers at all with a diploma in special education. A relatively low proportion of teachers with training in special educational needs was also found in a national survey of EBD facilities (Cooper and others, 1990). However, the maintained residential sector (Schools 3 and 4) did not appear to have a greater proportion of teachers with further qualifications, in contrast to the national survey. Nonetheless, the Head of School 4 referred to three teachers, in addition to one with a diploma, who had some relevant training and experience in special needs.

Opinions about the availability of adequate child care staffs varied. There were no complaints at School 1 and School 2. At the latter, it was acknowledged that providing cover in dispersed units was expensive. It was in the LEA schools that problems were experienced in attracting quality staff. At School 3 it was pointed out that there was no cover for care staff absence and demands on staff had substantially increased of late. At School 4 the status and salaries of staff were highlighted as problematic. Staffing ratios differed, with School 2 offering, in global terms, almost one-to-one care compared with School 3, where there were in all over three children to each member of care staff. School 4, where the ratio was approximately two-to-one, and School 1, where it was almost three-to-one, fell in between these extremes. Because of shift patterns, of course, not all of these would be working at any one time.

It was clear that none of the schools demanded formal qualifications from care staff. One Head put the position ironically, saying, 'We take people off the street'. In practice there were differences in actual levels of qualification.

Table 3.3   Child care staff and their qualifications

	School 1	School 2	School 3	School 4
Care staff	12	25	18	24
Certificate in Social Services	0	3	2	0
CQSW	0	1	0	0
Certificate in the Residential Care of Children and Young People	0	5	0	0
Teaching Qualification	2	1	1	0
State Registered Nurse	0	1	0	0
Nursery Nurse	0	0	1	1
Qualification in Youth Work	1	0	0	0
Qualification in Community Work	0	1	0	0

While the Head of School 2 was conscious of a relatively high level of qualification among care staff, his counterpart in School 3 was adamant that pay rates were too low to recruit qualified staff, even up to Head of Care. Nor was it easy according to the Head of School 4 to secure staff with the right personal qualities.

Given the problem of recruiting qualified staff for care duties, in-service training was obviously critical. At School 1, a special induction and training package was delivered, though not without hiccups in supply. Short courses were also available. Similarly, School 2 had access to short courses and, in particular, to the Open University introductory course for residential child care – P653. School 3 had appointed its only available social work qualified staff member to act as a training officer and provided two sessions a week training. Only one training day per year was formally available to care staff, but seven staff had undertaken the In Service Course in Social Care. At School 4, a number of care staff were attending inservice courses and all staff received in-house training for five days a year but lack of money was a fundamental obstacle. A common complaint was the lack of cover for care staff training, compared with teacher inservice training. However, the relatively favourable position of teachers was qualified at School 2 where teachers' access to courses depended on whether others had not occupied places beforehand.

The availability of particular external specialists has been a standard expectation in special education for 'difficult' children. Traditionally, psychiatry has usually been available in such schools. However, psychology has been more in evidence in the maintained sector and a shortage of help from psychotherapists and school social workers has been reported (Dawson, 1980). In Schools 1 and 2, a psychiatrist and a psychologist were available to work with children. At School 2, indeed, the psychiatrist was able to help with team-building. At School 3, however, these resources were felt to be in very short supply. Unlike the others, School 4 would, as a matter of policy, not seek psychiatric help, preferring psychological advice instead. Schools 1 and 2 could also call on other specialised therapeutic assistance, including play specialists. Two of the Heads complained, however, about the general problem of access to speech therapy.

Provision for health needs again showed some differences among schools. The LEA schools drew on the service of a specific nurse or matron, in addition to the general practitioner engaged by each school. These differences may be relevant in examining children's health outcomes at a later stage. However, having completed this examination of school resources, we now can turn to the internal management process.

How was the school policy shaped and turned into practice? One important method was to write a staff manual detailing a range of procedures. This was integrated into school development plans and curriculum documents. Regular meetings of senior staff reviewed current practice. At School 1, as previously indicated, management 'from above' was more evident. However, this school was unique in setting up a School Council representing children which met six times a year.

Supervision was evidently a principal means of turning policy into practice. Each Head lived on or very close to the school site, making possible what one called 'management by walking about'. Appraisal and review were also methods of checking on the application of policy. The interpretation of written rules was an extra responsibility which sometimes posed difficulties for senior staff. Regular briefings and staff meetings were felt to be useful in communicating policy, contributing to the staff's 'ownership' of policy, as one Head put it. Staff views could be represented through the regular meetings or through personal contact with the Head.

Schools varied in their reliance on formal supervision. School 2 required a three-weekly supervision session and annual appraisal but placed emphasis on the informal side of supervision. School 1 had only recently introduced formal individual supervision; it utilised paper reports based on standard checklists. At School 4, supervisory meetings took place on a weekly basis. At Schools 1 and 3, the praise and celebration of good work was regarded as of central value in supervision. This theme of praise was also linked to the staff's personal needs by School 4. In general, it was held that supervisors had some responsibility to alleviate staff's feelings of stress but it was also possible to do this by team-building and the encouragement of humour, or, on the other hand, by careful recruitment and staff's personal commitment to alleviate their stress.

One way of ensuring that consistent standards are applied is to integrate the work of different disciplines. Co-working was often possible in that teachers regularly performed care tasks. These were known as 'extraneous duties', though in School 2 it was emphasised that teachers' contributions were voluntary. In Schools 3 and 4, it was also possible for care staff to work in the classroom. Full team meetings were most frequent in School 1 where weekly gatherings took place; elsewhere, a schedule of approximately monthly meetings was common, though smaller interdisciplinary meetings took place more frequently at School 4. Mingling at assembly time gave another opportunity for contact.

Some general principles of work with children have been highlighted by legislation. In particular, the ideas of partnership with families and of Equal Opportunities have received legislative endorsement not only within educational legislation but within the Children Act 1989. How far did the schools acknowledge these principles?

Partnership with families was indeed accepted as a fundamental principle. Joint responsibility with parents was meant to be established from the beginning. Parents were welcome to visit the school and were helped with transport if necessary, though active parental interest was rare. Staff, for their part, could keep parents informed by telephone. At School 2, however, telephone contact with the separate units was said to be difficult. Mail for children posed dilemmas: at School 1, mail opening was supervised so as to uncover forbidden items. Formal progress reviews provided, however, a further opportunity for direct contact with parents.

Support was offered to parents through home visits, developing programmes in the home for the child or giving respite to parents by bringing children back to school. School 1 asked parents to report about children's behaviour 'on leave' and what help the parents could obtain for themselves. At School 2, a commitment to family work was recognised to be expensive in social work resources (possibly bearing in mind the distances between home and school); nonetheless, it might range from monthly visits to daily support. At Schools 2 and 4, work with parents was, however, described as limited, compared with what was desirable. School 3 had employed a single Home-School Liaison Officer but now acknowledged a need for direct contact with care staff.

Providing equal opportunities for both boys and girls has been an accepted aim of policy. But on these grounds coeducation also has its critics. It has been found to leave girls with insufficient attention from teachers and vulnerable to disruption by boys (Deem, 1984).

The mixing of girls and boys was not regarded as disadvantageous or a source of major problems. It was accepted as part of the creation of a normal environment. Equal opportunities for girls and boys were felt to be secured by open access to all activities, ranging from home economics to woodwork. On a more up to date note, Schools 1 and 3 were keen to give girls access to Information Technology. Unlike School 1, School 2 had a written equal opportunities policy framed by the organisation of which it was a part, while School 3 was also bound by a local authority policy. Though it did not have a written policy, School 4 described an equal opportunities review it had successfully conducted.

One serious question mark was raised by the Head of School 2 who felt that school activities were polarised between 'macho' sports and 'feminine' pursuits, creating an unfortunate vacuum in between. By contrast, the success of girls in the school football team was hailed as a sign of progress in School 4.

The living arrangements in a coeducational setting were not considered problematic. There was a viewpoint that co-residence amounted to a positive recognition of children's sexuality. But this did not prevent arrangements for locking or alarming doors that stood between girls' and boys' bedrooms. At School 3, in particular, there was a separate girls' unit as well as a mixed leavers' unit.

The education of children from minority ethnic groups has recently been the focus of several concerns, not least about aspects of the National Curriculum (Tomlinson, 1992). The treatment of children from minority ethnic groups was described variously in terms of providing access to the same curriculum, offering forms of specialised care, such as skin care or health care, or enabling access to cultural events, such as Barmitzvah. A policy statement on customs, diet and religion was binding in School 1. At School 2, multicultural studies on particular topics were offered to a mainly white pupil population, some of whom were admittedly felt to be racist. The Head of School 4 saw racism as a topic for Humanities, rather than for 'multiracial' education. At School 3, there was said to be a 'minority ethnic pressure group' as well as a 'religious' pressure group among staff, but progress could occur only at the pace of 'the slowest'. In indicating divisions among staff, this was a rather disappointing comment. Racism inside the schools was not, however, identified as a major concern by Heads. Surprisingly, anti-racist issues in education did not come to the fore in discussion with Heads, despite the research that shows the disproportionate number of children from some minority ethnic groups in EBD schools (Cooper and others, 1991). As we shall see in looking at referral policy, there appeared to be little opportunity, at the admission stage, for reflection and reappraisal of the composition of the school's intake.

Disability of a more general kind than emotional and behavioural difficulty was not seen generally as a bar to admission. The importance of disability awareness was stressed at School 1. However, in one respect there were limitations to what could be offered. In School 2, it was conceded that the buildings were not adapted to wheelchair use and this non-adaptation appeared to be the norm elsewhere. At School 4 the importance of obtaining specialist advice and support for disabled children was stressed.

In summary, the principles of coeducation and equal treatment were upheld and some important questions were addressed by the schools but no evidence was volunteered about attempts to monitor the progress of girls or minority groups – arguably a prerequisite for comprehensive equal opportunities practice.

Child care

The care of children with emotional and behavioural difficulties creates varied demands (Barratt, 1989). Part of it is concerned with generating an appropriate environment, part with social routines and skills, part with appropriate personal attention, including respect for children's privacy.

Written policies for care were general, though at School 1 these were perceived to focus on routines. School 3 was contributing to a local authority policy initiative which would fill a previous gap. Assessment was generally regarded as an important task. One Head suggested that the children's statements of special educational need were not informative about the care they required. Hence, a significant responsibility to assess children's concrete requirements fell on the schools.

Building self-esteem and a good self-image were common goals for children. At School 1, new and successful experiences, supported by good role models and praise, were instruments to this end. However, questions of identity were not always explored, as was explained at School 4, for example. In contrast, School 2 was committed to help children explore their life stories, as well as providing a caring environment. The Head of School 3 emphasised individual relationships with children but cautioned against 'forcing' them on the reluctant. It appeared that School 2 was more attuned to questions of identity and personal regard; other schools with lower proportions of children in care were more committed to an 'achievement' model (Wilson and Evans, 1980).

Personal and social relationships were addressed in various ways. Aspects of children's sexuality were featured in the academic as well as the care programme of schools. For example, School 3 had organised whole-school events with role play and group discussion on subjects such as AIDS. In terms of the school's practical care, it was important to encourage friendships, differentiating inquisitiveness from abusive or dangerous behaviour. Work in promoting friendships more generally was also encouraged in the schools. Pointing out the need to look beyond first appearances was stressed by the Head of School 1. Friendships outside the school, through attending clubs, for example, were promoted by School 2. The Head of School 3 wished children to avoid the temptations of peer delinquency and scrutinised friendships accordingly. At School 4, the social skills programmes which included positive peer culture, were described, however, as insufficient.

Asked about training in life skills, the Head of School 1 pointed to skills of negotiation and coping. School 2 also listed in a manual the practical skills that should be taught. Skills for future independence were regarded as important at School 3. At School 4 competence in a range of tasks assisted children to move to the next house. Development of personal interests was seen as part of the change process. At School 4 it was deliberately encouraged in the second and third houses.

Active social experiences are felt to provide children with an improved sense of well-being. Schools tried to offer such experiences by trips and activities or through contact with youth organisations. Contact with colleges or other schools was emphasised at School 3. School 2 had a considerable investment in outdoor pursuits, while other schools had access to similar facilities.

In three of the schools, each child was given a 'personal tutor' or 'key worker'. At School 3, no such person was formally nominated and there was no policy on allocating counselling time to individuals. By comparison, School 2 expected a weekly session and School 4 one session every fortnight. Arising partly from the experience of the research project, School 3 planned to introduce independent visitors, a scheme echoed by School 1, for example. In School 4, volunteer helpers with reading were perceived as 'sounding-boards' for children.

Child protection in residential schools has become a source of anxiety in recent years. It is now expected that a school should have a person responsible for coordinating child care procedures. In School 1 this was the Head himself, assisted by the Deputy. The Head also assumed responsibility in School 3 while in Schools 2 and 4 it was the Deputy. In the later chapter on children's progress, there is a discussion of the extent to which children were reported by staff to have undergone abusive experiences in a variety of contexts while on the school roll, confirming indeed the significance of this coordinating responsibility.

Curriculum

Curriculum development for EBD children has become a growing topic of interest, with the subsiding of the idea that emotional problems must take precedence (Wilson and Evans, 1980; HMI, 1989). However, any suggestion that teaching these children is straightforward has been challenged (Laslett, 1983). Evidence was therefore sought about policies and curriculum design.

Curriculum documents were in existence or in preparation in each school. Modifications were necessary, for example, to allow for the skills of new staff. Teachers' contributions to the curriculum were also supplemented at School 2 by care staff. Clearly, Heads' views on the curriculum were crucial. Their comments on education were particularly revealing, in that it was not necessarily seen as the primary focus. Ameliorating problems, for example, was one key aim, and education played its part. A conception of facilitating growth led the Head of School 2 to state that the whole activity of the school was child care in that sense. In practice, Heads tended to delegate responsibility for the classroom curriculum to their Deputies. It appeared that the Head operated as a coordinator and not as a direct educational supervisor.

The importance of the National Curriculum in EBD special schools has been acknowledged in a recent school survey where headteachers broadly welcomed its introduction (Davies and Landman, 1991). It was a powerful influence for change in each school, whether or not in the public sector. There were no suggestions that formal exemptions would be sought for individual children. The Heads of Schools 2 and 4 admitted some difficulties in offering a foreign language. Music too appeared hard to provide. At School 3, where learning difficulties featured strongly, there were anxieties about the future of assessment; here, nonetheless, improvements in basic reading skills had been targeted through extra sessions in school and in the home units.

The National Curriculum brings with it a preoccupation with subject teaching and assessment. On the other hand, special education has also been characterised by an interest in themes and topics. At School 1 a thematic focus was preferred to topic work. Topics and subjects were felt at School 2 to need balancing. At School 3, Humanities, Drama, Music and Art were all delivered through topics but Health Education and Information Technology were taught like the core subjects. Subject teachers were regarded at School 4 as best able to produce worthwhile topics.

Organising teaching and assessment to provide attainable goals can take the form of modules. At School 1 there were 15 modules in the Humanities Curriculum. Here the use of modules was felt to depend on the child, but in School 2 a modular approach was definitely preferred. Certificates other than GCSE were set as the main targets, though some GCSE entries were made at these schools. School 1 also used examinations set by the Associated Examining Board. Commitment to GCSE was strongest at School 4 where entry was commonplace, though all children were expected to obtain some form of certificate. School 3, which was designed to take children with moderate learning difficulties, did not currently enter children for GCSE though this was not considered impossible. Here also, modular assessment took place. Schools were therefore concerned to broaden their curriculum but at the same time to address pupils' learning through a range of strategies that differed somewhat in emphasis. These also included alternative forms of certified achievement to the conventional GCSE.

The learning environment and experienced teachers make contributions to children's progress. A mixed picture emerged from the comments. At School 1 the delivery of Craft and Information Technology was felt to need upgrading but there was a continuity of teaching staff experience. The learning environment of School 2 was not considered satisfactory in its design; but here the input of 'new blood' was welcomed. The Head of School 3 was dissatisfied with the provision of furniture as well as of books and materials but was pleased with the networked computing system. Though not so enamoured with new technology, the Head of School 4 emphasised its availability to pupils and felt satisfied with the school classrooms. He pointed to the diverse length of staff's experience. An interesting sidelight on the academic emphases of the schools came from discussions about homework. At School 1 it was optional but at least one session per week was expected. At School 2, homework depended on the child. Similarly, School 3 encouraged voluntary reading and it was noted that some children asked for homework. But at School 4, homework was set on no less than four nights of the week. These issues were explored in more detail in the assessment of children's progress discussed in a later chapter of the present study.

Maximising the relevance of the curriculum to children's futures especially highlights work experience and careers education, in conjunction with personal and social education. Prospects of employment for children in care are known to be bleak (Stein and Carey, 1986; Garnett, 1992). While there is some evidence that, in the past, children leaving schools for the 'maladjusted' have been able to find employment, special education is often associated with an unrewarding future (Dawson, 1980;

Tomlinson, 1982). School 1 offered a total of five weeks' work experience while School 2 could provide anything from one to six placements in the final year, occupying a considerable proportion of that period. Schools 3 and 4 appeared less ambitious, the former providing one to 14 days and the latter a standard fortnight. The difference in arrangements corresponded therefore with the division between the LEA and other schools. Each school had a careers teacher and was linked to the local careers guidance office. In preparing for the future, personal and social education was seen as a subject that crossed the boundary between the units and school. As the Head of School 3 put it, the point was to coordinate what was said in school and in the units.

Control

Defining behaviour that required control was a task that appeared to be differently interpreted. For School 1, it meant orderliness, reasonableness, good relationships and respect for people and property. At Schools 1, 2 and 3, there was scope for differences in what was expected of individuals. At School 2 it was possible to tolerate misbehaviour inside the school though control remained a priority. A range of tolerable behaviour needed to be communicated by staff to the child. Particular behaviours, such as absconding or swearing at teachers, did not necessarily attract penalties, depending on circumstances. At School 3, differences were made systematic by setting personal targets. Here, it was the appropriateness of the behaviour to the situation that had to be judged. The definition favoured by School 4 referred to behaviour that was helpful to individual survival in a social setting. Here disagreements among staff rather than attitudes to individuals were seen as leading to variations in control. Great store was set on standardisation, consistency and predictability, in contrast with other schools.

The formulation of a school disciplinary policy was a matter for staff; children played little or no part. The traditional ideal of self-government had no support (Bridgeland, 1971). Once again the management of the school was a major influence on School 1's policy, though at School 2 and 3 all staff contributed to policy and this was also true of senior staff at School 4. At School 1 there was a list of permitted sanctions. Damage to property was usually dealt with by fines, for example. School 2 also had a list of permissible and impermissible sanctions, involving deprivation of privileges. At School 3, children were sometimes confined to their units or denied 'treats' like a day out. It was not clear whether these were controlled by a policy. Sanctions at School 4 were related to the behavioural programme and, in the case of the token economy, were issued like tickets. Refusing a fine was itself penalised.

Policies on the control of children have been affected by the introduction of guidance associated with the Children Act 1989, which forbids restriction of liberty other than in secure accommodation and bans forms of degrading treatment. The application of the Children Act to a wide range of settings including schools has sharpened the attention paid to those institutions that take disturbed and disturbing children. In particular the legitimate physical restraint of children has been confined to situations when there is a danger to the child, other people or property (Department of Health, 1991 and 1993). In each school restraint of children was subject to written guidance and incidents were routinely recorded.

At School 4, it was clear that the Children Act had brought a very direct challenge to existing practice. Previously, it had been school policy that, after persuasion had failed, children showing hostile and negative behaviour would be made to comply with staff demands. This certainly meant overcoming resistance by physical means. It also meant securing compliance with ordinary features of the daily regime – going to school, washing hands, going to bed, and so on. By the standards of the Children Act restraint in such circumstances could not be upheld. However, in practice, this was not an issue simply confined to one school, as we shall discuss later. The regulations on treatment of children had also led School 4 to avoid another practice occasionally used in the past – dressing persistent absconders in 'PE kit'.

One consequence of the change in regime at School 4 was reported to be the first use of permanent suspension. A few instances of exclusion were also found at other schools. For Schools 2 and 3, a key criterion was the dangerousness of behaviour, ranging from arson (cited by School 2) to absconding (cited by School 3). Instances at School 1 were reported which involved a series of incidents, for example, breaking bounds, inappropriate sexual behaviour, climbing onto roofs to enter girls' bedrooms, destruction and aggression. These examples seemed to draw attention to a rather different aspect of teachers' perceptions and decisions – the escalation of misbehaviour (Galloway and others, 1982). Schools' use of exclusion is a vitally important question for further exploration, given the frequency among admissions of children with a history of residential special schooling. Ominously, it was pointed out at School 2 that excluded children had moved on to secure units.

Admissions policy

Referring cases to schools may have involved informal as well as formal channels. School 1 was sometimes approached by parents, as well as by its senior management or by local authorities. Referrals to School 2 were very much instigated by educational professionals or social workers responsible for cases which had been statemented but where placements were failing. In the LEA sector the central administrative process was dominant though talks with professionals did take place, indeed at School 3 in most cases. A more diverse process of referral appeared to be in evidence in the non-LEA schools.

Heads were asked what might be considered an inappropriate referral. How this question was answered clearly has a bearing on the mix of children in the school, and on the characteristics of our study samples. School 1 placed some restrictions on its admissions, refusing cases of serious arson, sexual offences, serious drug abuse and severe learning difficulties. Indeed this school had the lowest average rate of disturbing behaviours per pupil in the admissions sample. The Head of School 2 had strong reservations about only two categories of referral – those with physical handicap, specifically wheelchair users, and children described as 'acting-out recidivists'. Nonetheless, School 2 had the highest average rate of disturbing behaviour per pupil in the admissions sample and also the highest average rate of physical problems. The admissions policy was of comparatively limited scope, therefore.

At School 3, mainstream schools that simply wanted to rid themselves of troublesome pupils would find their referrals blocked. There was a concern too about aggressive children entering the school. This school's average rate of disturbing behaviour was somewhat above that in School 1 but it had marginally the lowest average rate of educational behaviour problems among its admissions. In the latter, rather than the former, respect, its policy seemed to have had some success.

School 4 had the most open policy, regarding no referral as in principle inappropriate. However, it would need to establish links with teachers or advisers in cases of particular special educational need. The school's admissions ranked second in average disturbing behaviours and first in educational behaviour problems but it admitted children with the lowest rates of physical problems and impairments. Here the supply of cases tended to lead towards the admission of certain categories of difficulty. There appeared to be no general unwillingness to accept children from health settings, such as hospital schools or psychiatric units. Indeed it was pointed out, rather surprisingly, that over 80 per cent of children at School 3 were receiving some form of medication full-time!

Most of the schools had a conception of an extremely disruptive child whose referral would be unacceptable and each was aware of some limitations on what could be offered to cater for particular needs. But, very clearly, a broad and diverse range of difficulty could be accommodated and there seemed to be no explicit mechanism at this stage for assessing combinations of difficulty that might be hard to deal with or better dealt with elsewhere. It appeared that the statementing process was largely taken for granted even though the type of boarding need had not been explicitly tested. When asked whether there was a possibility of a non-residential option at this stage, Heads were mostly doubtful. Only at School 3 was a day placement at the school possible in a special case.

Planning for children

To prepare for effective work, planning was necessary. Normally this was organised by a senior member of staff at the school. At School 2, LEAs took part in joint planning, but, at School 3, it was pointed out that psychologists were **not** normally involved. Question marks must be entered once more against these important transitional arrangements.

As children spend their time at the school, information is collected about them, which contributes to reviews and planning. Classroom testing was commonplace. At School 1 children's behaviour was graded on a weekly basis. Records of achievement had also been introduced (NEA, 1990).

At School 2, keyworkers completed personal profiles with the children at monthly intervals, dealing with topics like 'truthfulness' and 'attitude to authority'. Unit 'Logs' were also maintained.

School 3 made weekly assessments of progress on target skills. It had begun to assess children in National Curriculum subjects using computerised records of itemised skills that children could note. It was also committed to building up records of achievement with examples of a child's best work.

School 4 possessed records relating to Positive Peer Culture sessions, the token economy and so on, as well as 'House Logs' and records of tutorials. Interestingly, it also used sociograms, which require children's participation. In addition to classroom testing, it was enthusiastic about records of achievement.

Reviews usually took place every six months, though at School 4 it might be eight or nine months in practice and at School 3 it was an annual process. The level of participation by outside professionals was limited. While reports would be shared, participation varied, as at School 1 where children sometimes came from far afield.

Very often, you'll get nobody from a local authority attending or a local authority will ask, "Could we have all (our) reviews on one day?"

At School 3 it was very rare for a psychologist to take part in a review. Parental participation was normally encouraged: School 1 could offer some help with local transport; School 2's keyworkers would transport parents from their homes. Children's participation in reviews was also promoted in most cases. At School 1 children were asked to write their own reports and they attended reviews in full or often in part towards the end. However, at School 3 children were not always invited to reviews if there were complex issues, or surprisingly, if the review was positive! It was explained that children often could not accept praise and 'hold themselves together!' At School 4, children and parents were always expected to attend reviews. Finally, at reviews the schools committed themselves to action plans, that tutors or keyworkers were obliged to pursue. It appeared that schools had some way to go in making their review processes open and effective.

In order to shed light on children's intended progress within the schools, Heads were asked how they wished a child to perceive the school at an early, an intermediate, and a later stage. Answers were given which related closely to the ascribed ethos of the school. The Head of School 1 emphasised that initially the child should note an atmosphere of warmth and friendliness, mutual respect between pupils and staff, no unnecessary rules, and a respect for privacy. Similarly, at School 2, warmth, care and security were mentioned as initially important; the children should see that control did not mean rejection. At School 3, children should feel that their hands were being held. On a different note, the Head of School 4 felt that children should regard the school, at first, as 'tough but fair and decent'. As time passed, the schools hoped that the children would be looking for opportunity, for help to succeed, and for higher expectations. Progressively, children would begin to define their own positive goals, building on previous success.

Moving to a mainstream school was not, however, a major item on the agenda. The school were indeed prepared to give assistance to schools receiving former pupils as part of a reintegration process. A graduated process of induction could take place in those circumstances. At School 1, however, this type of transfer was not frequent. There was evidence in some schools outside the LEA sector that unplanned departures took place more frequently than transfers to some other form of provision. Indeed at School 1, there was evidence of 33 apparently unplanned departures within the period of more than four years during which the sample of 17 children was admitted. This compared with three transfers, each to a neighbouring residential EBD school. In the case of School 2, evidence of 16 unplanned departures was found over the corresponding period but, unfortunately, no transfers following review or reassessment took place. At School 3, 11 unplanned departures took place within a similar timescale. Here it was considered possible to achieve integration for an 11-year-old, but not for 14 or 15-year-olds. Mainstream schools were simply 'not interested'. In fact, during the period of three and a half years over which the sample was placed there, a total of 16 transfers were made to various forms of provision, following review or reassessment. A similar viewpoint was held by the Head of School 4, though help would be provided by the school to assist reintegration. In practice, there was no evidence of any planned transfers during the period of years when the children in the sample were placed at School 4. One factor here was the high average age of admission to the school; another was the difference between examination courses followed in special and mainstream schools. Unplanned departures, however, were very infrequent at School 4, amounting to only one case of permanent exclusion over the period in question.

Leaving school as the children grew up presented another challenge. A leavers' programme was in place at School 1 and there were plans for a post-16 leavers' unit to teach life skills and to prepare children for the National Vocational Qualifications. School 2 had developed a separate 'independence' unit with an extended programme of work experience. Its leaving procedure included a general case conference to plan for the future. A similar unit had been started at School 3. Post-16 provision was also being made there. At School 4 the senior unit was the nearest equivalent to a leavers' unit, promoting some 'independent' life skills. Schools were not, however, responsible for aftercare, though in some cases they were able to respond to leavers' telephone calls. While schools were acknowledging children's transition to a new environment and new responsibilities, it was not always evident how the transition was to be managed in individual cases. The law was changed in 1989 in order to strengthen provision for young people with special educational needs who had left school. However, the development of post-16 provision in these schools pointed to unmet need at this stage in children's lives. Clearly, with the emphasis of the Children Act 1989 on a guided transition to 'independence', this phase must assume increasingly great importance throughout the special educational needs sector.

In summarising what made these schools distinctive, the Heads drew attention to the 24 hours of care and education offered, to the emotional and social dimensions of care, to the possibility of change in behaviour through consistent attention and motivation, and to material benefits. These were key distinctions from what a day special school would offer. In looking at what made their own school distinctive, the Heads gave characteristic replies: at School 1, it was the stable, family atmosphere; at School 2, it was attention to individual needs and coping with challenging behaviour; at School 3, it was the celebration of achievement and raising of self-esteem; at School 4, it was the efficient change of behaviour, within ethical limits.

Among the essential ingredients for success, there was a generally high valuation of quality staff committed to the schools' goals. Yet, as previously indicated, staffing was not unproblematic. Interestingly, specialist input was not mentioned. Apart from a good environment, there was also a recognition of the need for clarity, consistency, stimulation and for records of achievement. But Heads with otherwise contrasting perspectives both drew attention to the child's viewpoint: the Head of School 2 emphasised cooperation, the Head of School 4, motivation.

The evidence, taken together, suggested that Heads were strongly influential in the development of school policy, drawing on a range of different philosophical premises to legitimate their power. In the independent and non-maintained sector, management systems external to the school were also powerful. Nonetheless, those in charge of the school were obliged to work within frameworks of resources and set objectives, such as the curriculum, which formed limits to their power. By contrast, children and parents had a restricted scope of influence.

Summary

- Children and parents appeared to have little influence on the policy of the schools, though in one a School Council had been organised.
- The system of accountability for Heads normally placed a substantial responsibility on them to define the school ethos. But in the private sector one school was subject to a broad management policy.
- Heads tended to have distinctive ideas about the intended ethos of the school and elaborated an individual philosophy which supported their ideas about practice. Their ideas differed partly in emphasis but also, and more crucially, in principle. One major strand drew on behavioural ideas about treatment and change. The alternative key influence was a philosophy of personal growth and development. While some leaned fairly clearly to one set of ideas, distinctly different emphases emerged in the behavioural camp. In addition, we found a clear example of an eclectic approach. The design of the schools corresponded with these ideas.

Since it was an aim of the research to compare a range of approaches, these differences were to be expected. What is important is the extent to which they may have had consequences for children's progress.

- Schools were open to referrals from any location over a large distance. Hence transport was a major undertaking for schools taking children from outside their area.
- Accommodation was regarded as unsatisfactory only in School 3. Library facilities and specialised resources like Science appeared more problematic in smaller schools outside the LEA sector.
- Classroom assistants varied significantly in background and availability to meet need.
- Care staff numbers and qualifications varied among the schools, with School 2 the most and School 3 the least generously resourced. Out of all 79 care staff, only one had a CQSW and five a Certificate in Social Services.
- Unlike other schools, School 3 could not make accessible sufficient psychiatric care for children, while School 4 chose not to use that resource at all.
- School policies were incorporated into documents.
- Systems of supervision, appraisal and review were in operation at each school.
- Interdisciplinary working was common to the schools.
- The principle of partnership with families was pursued through establishing opportunities for contact. However, even where there was a higher level of staff resource, as at School 2, work with families was acknowledged to be limited.
- Coeducation was defended as a principle and in practice, though curriculum issues were not addressed always in a thorough way.
- Attention to the needs of young people from minority ethnic groups was expressed in particular ways, in terms of care, while full integration was sought in school. The place of 'multicultural' studies differed among schools.
- Procedures for monitoring progress in terms of equal opportunities in general were not clear-cut.
- Care arrangements were defined in written documents.
- Regardless of the process of statementing, it was necessary to conduct fresh assessments of children's care needs at admission.
- Schools were more frequently oriented to building self-esteem by achievement than to resolving questions of identity. Attention to developing personal and social skills, interests and relationships was also seen as necessary.

- Personal tutorial arrangements had been established in each case except School 3. Here the school was set to follow the example of School 1 in appointing independent visitors.
- Curriculum matters were often delegated to a Deputy.
- The National Curriculum exerted a significant influence but topic teaching and modules were still seen as important methods of curriculum delivery.
- There were some complaints about educational resources but no strong views were expressed about the relevance of staff's experience.
- Work experience was provided in greater quantity in the private sector.
- A range of responses to misbehaviour was found and highly predictable sanctions were favoured only in School 4.
- The use of physical restraint had been influenced by the guidance associated with the Children Act 1989.
- Admissions policies made some impact on the composition of the school population but not in a systematic way.
- The level of participation by outside professionals in the planning and review process was distinctly limited.
- Transition to the world outside the school did not appear to be generally subject to definite planning mechanisms; in some schools transfers to other provision were less frequent than unplanned departures, though programmes for leavers were established at the schools in some form.

4. The practice of residential schooling

Systems of schooling can be planned on paper but, to be realised, they require a series of practical conditions to be fulfilled. When a teacher enters a classroom, for example, what happens is a product not merely of the resources provided by a system but also of an interaction with the children themselves. To understand the way in which a system works in practice, some evidence of its operation at the micro-level is needed. In order to gain some insight into the daily practice of the schools, visits were made that entailed classroom observations in each for three days, as well as a series of subsequent visits in which the details of daily living were experienced at first hand. In the course of these visits, which were also occupied with interviewing and examining documents, 49 overnight stays took place. We begin by looking briefly at the evidence of classroom visits in each school.

Observations of lessons

Research on schools has sought to identify those qualities that are associated with effective teaching and learning. However, those highlighted by research vary in their degree of specificity and relevance. For example, if tasks are to be both 'realistic' and 'challenging', pupils' learning stages will need to be precisely assessed; if expectations are to be 'high', just how high (Ainscow, 1991)? With this proviso in mind, there are some very general concepts that research has endorsed. These include the ideas of an 'instructional focus', an orderly climate, and positive expectations. Research on classroom discipline has repeatedly emphasised the value of praise and found punishment ineffective (Johnstone and Munn, 1987). In addition behavioural theory has recommended key principles: rule-setting; systematically withdrawing attention from, that is, **ignoring** infractions; and praising conformity (O'Leary and O'Leary, 1976). Overt and intrusive control is not associated with effective discipline (Reynolds, 1975). In order to examine these themes in schools' practice, the researcher in effect took a snapshot of various lessons, attending them and filling in a detailed checklist afterwards.

School 1

The substance of teaching at School 1 held a clear educational focus, influenced especially by preparation for tests and examinations as well as other future educational events. Basic educational skills like spelling were tested. This gave a sense of purpose and a forward-looking momentum to classwork. It was common to introduce the group to a standard activity, supported by an appropriate set of materials (such as worksheets). Some classes were almost wholly taken up with individual work. Typically, teachers gave brief individual assistance to pupils and there were also episodes when teachers and pupils were engaged in clarifying aspects of the task. On several occasions the classes took ten to 15 minutes to settle, however.

A senior staff member was prolific in praising performance but this was not a frequent strategy in other classes. One child was promised the chance of reading a comic for a short period if he did some work. Teachers tended to give commands or reproofs when they noticed unacceptable behaviour, such as holding paper conspiratorially in front of the face or swearing. One wandering child was guided with a hand back to her place. Poor behaviour was evidently ignored on a few occasions. Talking while engaged in manual tasks was not disapproved.

There were during the week of observation three individuals (two boys and one girl) who openly refused to work on a consistent basis. Disruptive individuals were managed at School 1 by withdrawing them from class or transferring them to another class to do set work; classroom assistants were available to accompany them, and care staff would guide wanderers into class. The school therefore offered increased individual attention to disruptives, rather than ignoring or penalising their behaviour. The majority of children were willing to work and followed what they were asked to do. Indeed, in long double periods on individual tasks, their apparent perseverance was remarkable. There was some evidence that the quieter girls and boys were unable to call on as much teacher attention as the more articulate or disruptive. One boy also told the researcher privately how easy the work was and how 'bad' one of the disruptive boys was. The extent to which children from minority ethnic groups benefited from classroom practice was also a focus for research observations. A number of the four black boys observed were certainly capable of demanding teacher attention though none belonged to the consistently disruptive group. The researcher was shown embroidery by black boys, which appeared to show how the curriculum was integrated.

At School 1, feedback to children was concentrated at the end of the school day in the assembly hall. In one such meeting, there was a quiet atmosphere. One child was tugging at her hair abstractedly. Girls and boys sat on chairs in separate groups, while staff were asked by a senior staff member to comment. Some individuals had apparently 'let themselves down'. A good deal of praise was, however, given to others. Children themselves made no input to the substantive meeting. There were, nonetheless, plenty of volunteers for a competition that involved a trip outside the school. This assembly lasted half an hour. The other main means of rewarding good behaviour was to give grades. The organiser of the scheme explained that she was aware of grading anomalies that needed attention.

To summarise, School 1 approached education with a clear sense of purpose and had planned for children's achievements. Most children were ready to respond to the curriculum and there were some 'safety valves' to deal with the few disruptive children. Teachers were patient and unthreatening and sought to carry through their lessons without interruption. However, the classic behavioural strategies in the classroom such as praise and 'ignoring' were not sharply evident and from that perspective much reliance was therefore placed on the assemblies and the grading system, which was under review.

School 2

Though it dealt with a secondary age group, the curriculum at School 2 was implemented through primary-style class teaching in the morning and a secondary curriculum in the afternoon. The use of class teaching had the effect of reducing traffic between classrooms, yet unwanted movement was still recognised as a problem. The walls of the classrooms were covered by children's personal board spaces and thus signalled their individual territory. Ironically, perhaps, the campus itself was one setting for the senior 'work experience' curriculum! Topic-based work was regarded as especially appropriate. A whole day could be set aside for a topic like 'China'.

Teaching in groups had to acknowledge different competences. One teacher explained that in a project on geography, two children might be able to measure, unlike the third, but they could be taught as a group. Observations suggested that individual tasks took precedence over presentations to groups. Formal objectives were not prominent during the week of observation, though a modular assessment for a certificate was witnessed. Clarification of the topic occurred in some lessons and there was a consistent pattern of help to individuals. When two girls arrived late from their unit, the teacher made them hot drinks. As at School 1, a senior staff member was most lavish in giving praise. Some ignoring of misbehaviour also took place. Reactions to disapproved behaviour like swearing tended to include an element of subtle mockery. This echoed the friendly relations that most teaching staff sought with children.

For example, one of the teachers allowed children to use his first name, used nicknames for them, and was not shy about giving them a friendly, appropriate touch on their arms. One boy was observed trying unsuccessfully to cadge money for cigarettes from the teacher. Another explained that in the afternoon a short period of quality work was expected. Overhearing this, a child said, 'You mean we don't want to work and you can't make us', resulting in laughter. Time on the computers playing games was given as a reward. It appeared consistent that tracksuits and trainers were acceptable wear for teachers.

Friendly relations did not prevent teachers from threatening to stop an activity or even making a report of unacceptable language. One problem was of dealing with children who interrupted other lessons. Teachers were asked to issue those leaving classes with notes of permission. However, one girl entered a class telling the teacher another child was on drugs and the teacher left to investigate, followed by the class, returning, relieved, a little later. Unlike School 1, there was not such visible support during school time from the staff of dispersed units. The detached living arrangements also led to some late arrivals for those children who were trusted to make their own way to the school site. Children were also withdrawn to attend various therapeutic settings. When children refused a lesson it was not always clear what arrangements were being made for them. While children broadly accepted the demands made upon them, there were tendencies among some to wander. In addition, one particular girl was prone to loss of temper, not helped by her provocative 'friend'. A further girl made occasional involuntary noises and swore at a boy, behaviour attributable to her neurological condition. At a later date, the school admitted a boy who exhibited disruptive and sometimes bizarre behaviours such as consciously making unusual noises and lying down after assembly.

The curriculum at School 2 was therefore designed to provide flexible scope for individual tasks. In this sense, children with a variety of difficulties could find their own niches. Friendly relations encouraged some degree of negotiation as well as limit-setting, but behavioural strategies were rare. The curriculum was not likely to be radically disrupted but it did not seem geared explicitly to achievement.

School 3
At School 3, there was a clear commitment to individual educational needs. Learning difficulties were accepted as the norm and three of the children

were considered to have difficulties that bordered on the severe. Individual tasks were normally arranged and group teaching appeared to be relatively infrequent. The focus seemed to lie on individual targets rather than any public certificates. The majority of classes settled quickly though it could take time to sort out that children were on the correct task. The instructional focus was usually specific to an individual pupil, and classes were not publicly directed in a way familiar in mainstream schools. However, team teaching was observed. When work in groups was conducted, it was oriented to a previous experience, allowing for the possibility of repetition of learning. Teachers routinely offered help to individuals as they circulated round the class and it was during this process that clarification of the task normally took place. It was at this school that children asked the researcher to listen to their reading, implying this was a crucially valuable skill for which any help was welcome. Care was shown when a pupil with a headache was advised to see the school nurse. Praise was not generally observed, except in the class for younger pupils.

A number of the classes appeared perfectly well-behaved. Patience was certainly a virtue here: one class experienced 110 consecutive minutes of individual reading. Some reproofs and commands were issued in response to impolite language. Ostentatious 'laziness' such as lying on a desk might be ignored. In one case, a child was reminded about the effect on his 'mark book' if he swore. Classroom targets were included in the weekly reward system. The system of individual tasks rewarded children for overt conformity but allowed them some licence, as when a child played games on the computer instead of going through a learning programme. Teachers were usually positive towards pupils, occasionally touching them in appropriate ways, but those children with particular needs for affection, who wanted hugs, would be pushed away by the teacher. Problems of discipline were noted outside the classroom at breaks.

Some positive attention was given to the minority of girls, in ensuring they used computers or learned how to use a hammer, but help was not always systematic. The girls in the school varied. They included one with borderline severe learning difficulties, who was pleased to show the researcher pictures of cats and dogs in a picture book, as well as a more able girl who felt aggrieved at the way her behaviours had been forcibly dealt with by a staff member. There were black boys and girls with a range of needs. One of the black boys began a fight outside the classroom after being called a 'nigger'. This was taken by staff to be a sign of progress because he did not usually recognise himself as black! It was not altogether clear how this interpretation was constructed. Nonetheless, it indicates an additional problem for black children faced with racist name calling, particularly in special schools (Troyna and Hatcher, 1992). This boy was allocated the school's classroom assistant but a member of care staff was also needed in one class. Observations suggested that it was among the children with highly specialised needs that classroom assistants might have been most usefully employed.

The school's work was concentrated on the implementation of a behavioural programme of assessment which took place weekly. Teachers moderated their individual assessments at a weekly meeting chaired by the Head. These were then combined with care staff assessments and the final assembly of the week took on a very positive air of celebration as awards were given to substantial proportions of children, culminating in the prized 'gold' awards for all-round success.

School 3 had adopted a behavioural philosophy and programme which gave a degree of focus to its highly individualised approach. The emphasis on individual work and skills tended to reward patient compliance and minimised the risk of individual disruption. However, children with highly specialised needs called for a marked degree of careful handling. It was outside the classroom that more tensions were observed.

School 4

School 4 had designed its curriculum clearly on secondary school lines. Subject teaching had become increasingly emphasised. A senior staff member explained that the National Curriculum with subject specialists had replaced class teachers for the teaching of Mathematics and English. The pre-eminence of the standard curriculum meant that children with learning difficulties were individually helped. For example, some extra reading assistance was given through withdrawal from the classroom. GCSEs were the target for many children, along with certificates in practical subjects. Classrooms were arranged formally with very neat and impersonal displays of work. Order and neatness were given a high priority. The children were expected to sit quietly for two minutes before morning assembly began and to line up on the playground before going to the classroom. Polished shoes were universally worn and trainers strictly kept out of the classroom. Children were normally settled promptly except on occasions when teachers were covering for colleagues and assignments had to be sorted out piecemeal. It was in these classes that some children showed signs of boredom. Individual tasks were an important component of classroom work but these included projects that gave continuity to children's efforts. One that called upon an interesting range of skills took the form of a school-based social survey! In the reception class, children were kept fully occupied with small scale assessment exercises. Classroom resources were felt by teachers of practical subjects to be insufficient.

Following behavioural assumptions, no less than 12 rules were posted in the reception classroom. Despite the formal ethos of the school there was a relationship between teachers and pupils that at times included expressions of warmth and humour. In the reception class, children sometimes had a choice of taped music as a background to work. Several minutes' help was normally provided to individuals doing classwork. Surprisingly, in view of the school's behavioural philosophy, praise was not frequently heard and was not observed in some classes at all. Since the school operated with a token economy, one major sanction was the withdrawal of a class point. In fact, the children behaved in acceptable ways very largely throughout the lessons observed. Conversation was tolerated especially during manual tasks. In general a few mild words were sufficient to exercise control. However, points were deducted on two occasions. On the first, a boy was penalised for lack of output. He protested that he had been withdrawn for help with reading. On the second, some children were asked to play the roles of inattentive students. As they did so, a half-ruler hit the floor. The teacher tried to find out who had thrown the ruler but no one admitted responsibility, despite the teacher's encouragement that it might have been an accident. Points were then withdrawn from the whole class until an admission was forthcoming. These sanctions produced resentment and abuse against one boy who was regarded as the likely culprit. This boy complained on other occasions of victimisation by staff and by pupils and his complaints were well-known to staff. The incidents illustrated the ways in which pressure on the group was used to control individuals. Encouragingly, there was no sign that girls or black children were treated differently in the classroom. It was noticeable by comparison with other schools that classroom assistants were not observed in the lessons. From this brief study, it appeared that such assistance was certainly not pivotal to classroom functioning.

We need however to look at the way classroom control was integrated into the general order of School 4. Apart from losing points, misbehaviour among members of a house unit at break time was also observed to lead to withdrawal of the whole unit from class for a period. A senior staff member later compromised on the resulting loss of points, confining the punishment to certain individuals who lost 'break points' (rather than lesson points also, as originally). Here the token economy was mechanically applied, again exploiting group pressure, before a more finely tuned sanction was produced. In justifying this process later in the classroom, the teacher gave the example of Underground passengers halted on a train during a bomb alert. Asked to think of similar examples, a boy acidly referred to his experience of being 'caught for shoplifting when I hadn't done it'. In this use of group pressure there were dubious implications for the practice of positive peer culture which is based on group assistance rather than sanctions. Withdrawal from class was also discussed at a teachers' meeting as a possible measure to deal with a misbehaving individual and there was agreement about the need for an 'isolation programme'.

In sum, School 4 was committed to National Curriculum objectives and to GCSE, giving special forms of assistance to children with learning difficulties. Its particular emphasis on order and neatness was backed by a highly structured behavioural system covering both care and education. Generally attentive pupils were observed, mainly working on individual tasks. However, group sanctions created the possibility of resentment and complaints of victimisation. The behavioural structure was also not the only source of sanctions, which included withdrawal from class.

The process of education

The processes occurring within classrooms at each school demonstrate that curriculum objectives varied from a GCSE-dominated approach in School 4 to more of a classic special education model in School 3. Alternative forms of certification, especially in the other schools, were an attempt to provide a public purpose to classroom work. There were few cases where the class resources did not meet the demands of the lesson. Classes were organised in ways that drew pupils' attention to their individual tasks and denied opportunities for disruption. The possibility of fully developing a cooperative style of learning, on the other hand, was not pursued.

A friendly and caring attitude was pronounced among teachers in School 2 but teachers in each school displayed patience, often gave individual help, and conveyed a positive attitude towards individuals. Nonetheless, praise was not a common feature of their classroom repertoire and this was so, even in schools with a strong behavioural philosophy. Instead there were usually a variety of **built-in** rewards which gave some support to teachers' efforts. In School 2, however, a great deal hinged on teachers' ability to exercise a personal influence. Schools depended in part on methods of withdrawing children from difficult situations. Whereas this might bring additional individual attention in some schools, it might, as in School 4, be described as a form of isolation. Only in School 4 did sanctions appear in any way controversial or divisive, though, as we have seen, public sanctions were not frequent occasions in the classrooms of any school.

There were signs that individual girls posed no less of a problem than boys. It was difficult on the basis of observations to see how the organisation of classroom practice might have influenced particular girls to behave as they did, though one girl at School 1 persisted in claiming that lessons were 'boring' and another at School 2 was upset because it was impossible to make pancakes in the food technology class on Shrove Tuesday. Children from minority ethnic groups did not appear to show particular patterns of opposition or conformity, though there was a disturbing case of racist name-calling at School 3. At School 1 some African-Caribbean boys were described as noisy because of 'their culture' – a comment which suggested that some behaviour problems among African-Caribbeans amounted to a clash with 'our' (white) culture.

We need also to be aware of some medically defined conditions that influence mood and behaviour, like epilepsy or Tourette's Syndrome (Graham, 1986). There were classrooms in which some children coped with conditions that affected their potential to respond to educational demands.

Classroom observations – albeit brief – were useful for the research in indicating the broad framework of practice within which teachers operated and children approached learning tasks. Curriculum objectives were varied in ways that make it difficult to identify an agreed instructional focus, in the sense used by research on school effectiveness. Indeed this may be a characteristic feature of special education as it has been organised up to now. Children's observed responses to the curriculum suggest that they had a potential for attentive learning. However it was not easy to determine that teachers' classroom techniques were 'special' in any obvious sense. Rather, it was the general organisation of the school with small classes and so on that appeared to make it 'special'. Thus, the structure of rewards and sanctions and the availability of support and facilities for withdrawal shaped the context for classroom practice in important ways.

Care and control

Having examined classroom practice, it is important to establish what is offered beyond its doors. Research on residential work in a variety of school settings has shown that care has been organised in different ways but that care which addresses fundamental problems, rather than secondary responses to separation from families, can be successful in reducing unwanted behaviour in the residential setting (Millham, 1987). As we shall see, the schools' efforts were directed at influencing behaviour through group care as well as individualised interventions. The idea of a curriculum for 24 hours was mooted by Heads. However, as group care situations are often felt to run the risk of being routinised so that children's individual needs are glossed over, the research paid particular attention to group interaction.

A number of opportunities arose for observation of non-classroom activities, especially in group situations. It was decided not to seek access to personal counselling sessions because there was a danger of invading privacy and any observations would doubtless influence what was said, thus negating the original purpose. However, information from documents such as staff logs and personal files shed light on general aspects of the school experience. Comments by staff also put some of these observations in context and a number of senior care staff were interviewed about general arrangements in their house or unit. These sources helped to fill out a picture of the children's daily experience and how it was managed by the different schools. In the following section, we shall look more closely at the accommodation provided by each school, the group activities offered, and the ways in which controls, including physical restraint, were applied.

Living arrangements

Living arrangements at School 1 were comfortable and reasonably private, though three dormitories, each for five children, were observed. Self-chosen pictures were attached to the walls and music equipment was visible and sometimes audible! Girls and boys had separate lounge areas but many activities were for mixed groups. The spacious park had room for sports activities and for the care of horses. There was access to the countryside and local villages. In general, School 1 appeared to be offering a rural boarding environment for all its children.

At School 2, living arrangements were also generally satisfactory, but the accommodation was organised into various units in different settings. A structured unit for boys was situated on campus next to the school block – ideal for supervision! There was a mixture of single and double bedrooms, and the design would allow for an intake of girls.

An 'independence unit' was located in a comfortable detached dwelling, officially for children at least 15 and a half-years-old, on a residential estate some miles away; here, children had single bedrooms but it would have been less easy to accommodate girls.

The mixed 'nurturing unit' occupied a large country house with extensive grounds. Living conditions in the 'nurturing unit' were comfortable with impressively furnished and decorated individual bedrooms, tidily kept and full of toys. Special playrooms were provided, in which life story scenes were reportedly played out. One girl, for example, was said to 'make' her Daddy, then kill him. Psychological advice was available to guide the work of staff. Part of the house had been divided to form a 'semi-independent' flatlet occupied by two older girls.

The purpose of these units was to cater for children's different needs in an appropriate domestic setting. Physical separation from the other children in non-school time was deliberate while some units were designed to slip invisibly into their normal residential environments. Apart from the 'nurturing' unit, School 2's provision lay very much in an urban setting. In this respect it differed from the other schools.

At School 3 the units were grouped on the main campus, though one of the units was accommodated in a separate part of the grounds. The living situation at School 3 appeared less obviously comfortable than at Schools 1 and 2. Bedrooms were not well decorated and some furnishings needed repair.

One boy felt that living in the more detached 'independence unit' was a definite improvement, however. In these respects, observations confirmed what the Head described as deficiencies in the material environment. Nonetheless, there was parkland, sports areas and access to local villages. Like School 1, School 3 offered a rural boarding experience but appeared less well-equipped to provide a good standard of comfort.

School 4 was located in its own parkland adjoining a small country town. Like School 2, School 4 had a planned approach to accommodation but on very different lines. Conditions at School 4 were governed by the hierarchy of living units, designed according to particular behavioural assumptions. In the lowest House the decoration was bare and no personal decorations or belongings had been allowed. Some children slept on bunk beds; there was one bedroom for five children, and others catering for between four and one. This regime was somewhat relaxed in the next House, so that teddy bears had been allowed there, for example. Further improvements were visible in the next two Houses, while in the top House there were individual bedrooms, a kitchen and a lounge with a sound system, a television set, a snooker table, and so on. Only recently had the conditions in the lowest House begun to improve.

School 4's arrangements were entirely determined by its conception of rewards. The assumption was that children would normally respond to their environment not by adapting to it but by seeking more rewarding environments within the school. Yet progress to the top House was not necessarily smooth and there appeared to be spare accommodation there.

Accommodation away from home raises questions about means of communication. At School 1 there were several opportunities to make phone calls. A weekly 'official' call home was facilitated but payphones were available at any time, preferably after six pm. These were placed on landings and were not entirely private but hoods were due to be installed. The numbers of *Childline* and a free 24-hour school counselling service were made available as well as those of a local panel of independent visitors. Pupils would nonetheless use the local telephone box which allowed them to reverse the charges, and, where this was known, it was not discouraged. At School 2 it was possible for children to use phones in their units; boys in the structured unit were also given money to use a public telephone box, in addition to an official weekly call home. At School 3, however, boys in one unit were told that they could make supervised use of a payphone but only twice a week. At School 4 the *Childline* number was posted but phones dedicated to children's use had not been installed. In the top House, children were signed out for trips to the phone box.

The organisation of living arrangements showed some of the diversity between schools, but indicated a lack of resources in School 3 only. We now turn to the experience of group care, drawing on various examples of activity outside school time.

Activities

During the evenings School 1 offered a full roster of several planned activities under staff supervision, which were open to all the children. In the following example we see how these elements were brought together in practice.

A summer activities evening at School 1 combined natural history and cricket, each run by a male member of the care staff. The two groups came together towards the end of the one and a half hours set aside. The mixed groups of children were seen to be active and occupied. The leader was very relaxed, lingering behind the children as they toured the grounds with a metal detector; as they progressed, a girl and a boy were heard debating which should use it. One girl walked arm in arm with the leader, as he combined attention to the group and to the individuals. One of the boys found a sick rabbit and carefully handed it round for inspection. Meanwhile, another boy showed off his karate skills with a pile of slates that he encountered; another, wishing to emulate him, found the experience more painful!

The cricket was more strongly guided with stern warnings to spectators to avoid flying balls. A girl with impressive batting skills was warmly approved. Staff approached their tasks with a positive and attentive attitude. Children were supervised with an awareness of their safety but with some leeway for exploration. The odd swear word was met with a brief 'Oy!'. Towards the end there were signs of assertive sexual approaches by boys. Two boys mounted the backs of girls in 'horseplay'. As one slapped a girls's bottom she was heard to say sarcastically, 'I'm not into bondage'. Meanwhile one of the other boys played with a girl who suddenly gave a reaction that implied that her breasts had been touched. The leader, observing this, made a disapproving comment. The whole episode was therefore conducted in a low-key style, with an attempt to draw a balance between control and laissez-faire. Caring, non-invasive physical contact with children was acceptable, but children's contact with one another was evidently scrutinised. Other examples bring out this point, drawn from the daily log to which all the staff had access.

A girl was recorded to have been upset at lunch break because she had been told by 'mixers' (rumour mongers) that her boyfriend had finished with her. She was told by a staff member that she had been known to 'mix and stir' and she should treat people equitably and think about who her real friends were. If this tale epitomises the strains of romance, another log report wrote about a couple 'frenching' (french-kissing) in the girls' toilet, discovered by information received from a child. Messages about trouble planned for the night-time were overheard in another instance, as they were shouted across to the girls' bedrooms. At bedtime, it was apparently usual for the girls to knock loudly on the dividing door. These examples testify to the combination of surveillance, guidance and policing that made coeducational residential settings manageable in the eyes of Heads. At School 1, the more open living situation intensified this feature.

School 1's style of care was therefore based on an integrated model in which relations between girls and boys were kept under observation and management. The evening activities were clearly meant to be educational. An educational plan, therefore, was influential throughout the school, though interactions in non-school time left some room for more personal needs to be addressed and for children to interact more freely.

In School 2, the different settings made it more difficult to identify a uniform objective. But these settings were related to conceptions of how to care for particular needs – young people preparing for 'independence', those needing supervision, and others requiring 'nurture'. Some impression of those differences can be given by selected observations which focus on children considered to require group supervision.

In the supervised and structured unit, evening activities were sometimes concerned with relaxing, but often with something more invigorating, such as swimming, bowling or outdoor activity. On one such evening, staff were engaged in relaxed group supervision but sometimes talked to individuals. The staffing level was designed to allow time for a talk between a keyworker and a child. Occasional signs of friendly disapproval were heard in response to swearing; praise was given to individuals who had abided by the rules about going out unsupervised, though one boy was kept on a curfew. In spite of the fact that smoking was permitted in one area, an attempt to take cigarettes upstairs was prevented. The children were active and occupied, although one boy was restlessly concerned both with his lack of pocket money and with finding an opportunity to smoke. Despite a reminder from a member of staff, one of the younger boys continued to watch a '15' certificate video. Staff approached their tasks with a degree of flexibility and indicated their expectations about behaviour concisely. They made themselves available to children, for example, by allowing them to enter the staff office freely.

An evening visit to the 'nurturing' unit revealed something of the day-to-day experience of this mixed unit in which, on this occasion, the girls presented particular difficulties. There was an underlying pattern of hostile gestures and remarks among some of the girls. While some of those signals were ignored, staff warned one child she might lose the chance to participate in an activity later. When a girl accused another of giving her 'dirty looks' at the tea table, she was taken from the dining room by a staff member to the kitchen and spoken with. This was a form of withdrawal which increased the individual attention to that child. This girl had been diagnosed as having a particularly striking and unusual neurological condition. She apologised to the researcher cheerfully later, saying she had earlier been upset because the researcher was not planning to speak individually with her (because the timing of her placement did not fall within the methodological framework of the study). Staff appeared unable to relax in the face of a mutually antagonistic atmosphere among the group, which apparently could not be left unsupervised. Exercising control was therefore a major priority, but in this case it was centred on giving individual attention.

The process of group supervision at School 2 was characterised by attempts to indicate behavioural expectations and to take action selectively and only when a limit had been reached. Individual attention was given where possible, but this seemed stretched in the case of the 'nurturing' unit. The provision of high staffing ratios in the units did not seem to be linked to a dramatic departure from ordinary caring. Rather, the staffing ratio appeared designed, in principle, to allow children to be cared for in as normal a manner as possible.

There was evidence in School 3 that the care task was differently perceived by care staff in key posts and that there was not a complete consensus about what constituted acceptable or appropriate practice. This disagreement extended to the treatment of children from minority ethnic groups and gave rise to strongly expressed views, for example, about the availability of culturally appropriate food. Indeed the Head referred, as we have seen, to 'lobbies' among staff. Such differences had implications for the leadership of the care dimension as a whole which needs more exploration than could be carried out during this research.

A home recreation night in a boys' unit at School 3 included playing pool, table football, computer games and listening to football on the radio. Computing was so popular that time on the unit's machine had to be rationed. Children were actively engaged by these activities, though some rumbustious behaviour was reprimanded. A smaller boy was rescued from another who had gripped him round his neck. On a happier note, the latter was counselled in a relaxed way about his transfer to the school's 'independence' unit and praised for talking about it. There was sensitivity to children's situations and an awareness of their interactions. It was not easy at School 3 to identify an explicit programme for children's leisure activities. In practice, the home units seemed to conduct their own activities or children 'played out', though some school facilities like the main computing room were accessible during the evening.

The experience of School 4's children was once again influenced by their status in the school, and, through the behavioural systems in use, by the choices which their assessed behaviour had given them. In the token economy applied in the two lower houses, each part of the day and each major routine activity was allocated a point. In the lowest House there were 26 opportunities in a 24 hours period to earn points by doing what was expected. Token expenditure was then possible on evening activities, trips out, tuckshop and 'video club', baths, and later bedtimes and, surprisingly, visits out of school with parents. Though parental visits to school were not restricted, weekend visits home were less frequent for children in lower houses; it was explained that resources did not permit every child to return home on each weekend. Though washing and showering were freely available, the use of baths and of parental contact as conditional rewards appears somewhat questionable under current guidance and regulations (Department of Health, 1991, p14, p66). Watching TV was restricted to once a week except for children ready to transfer to the next house.

Records were meticulously kept, allowing quantitative measures of compliance to be produced for reports. Scores were posted for children to see, along with score criteria. Supervision was kept especially tight in the lower houses; one care staff member explained that children were 'never let out of your sight'.

Transfer to a higher house unit was based on specific formulas for achieving given targets. For example, to move to the third house required over the previous five weeks the fulfilment of six absolute conditions – not causing night time disturbances, avoiding 'conflict', a satisfactory education score and so on – and four out of five other conditions – such as staying within 'supervision and control', and scoring more than a set number of tokens. Such conditions were effectively subject to policy review and thus to management discretion over the long term. Admission to the third house entitled children to go cycling, pony trekking, skating or camping. If inter-house progression was subject to complicated conditions, regression was not: smoking at camp, for example, led to return to the lowest house. In the top house, friends from outside the school were allowed, subject to staff and parents' approval. Visits to youth centres were encouraged. Greater freedom was therefore an important benefit, though house sanctions were still applicable and return to the lowest house remained possible.

Dining arrangements in School 4 illustrated the emphasis on order and routine, as well as differentiation. The lowest houses ate in an area resembling a small school canteen. The third house ate in a separate room nearby, with pot plants on the formica tables. In the top house, detached from the main building, meals were taken on a wooden table in a dining room.

Supervision of eating was stringent in each house (though this was also frequent in other schools). In addition children in the lower houses at the end of a meal were told to be silent, instructed to sit up straight and then made to wait in line before filing to their accommodation. If a child pushed another, the whole group was made to return.

Life in School 4 was therefore highly organised, supervised and regulated for the majority of children. The more informal methods used in other schools nonetheless called on close supervisory and interactive skills to set boundaries for behaviour and provide support. It was in School 3 that divergencies among staff appeared more evident.

Group sessions

In order to understand how schools develop children's social and personal skills, evidence was collected about group sessions. These varied from a School Council in School 1, a group work session in School 3 and several examples in School 4 of group sessions influenced by 'positive peer culture'. While the sessions differed in purpose they revealed the potential for such work with 'difficult' children.

In School 1 the Council was formed from pupil representatives and chaired by a senior member of the school staff. At the meeting observed, a suggestion that each child had an individual bar of soap was welcomed. The response to suggestions about going out without supervision and having later bedtimes was to consider them as rewards for good behaviour. Leaving children on their own in Woolworths was not fair to the 'compulsive stealers' in the school. A request for longer breaks was met by a reference to government requirements for a certain number of hours. Plastic bed sheets were queried by a representative but it was replied that 'some children do have accidents'.

It was clear that the School Council was approached by children in a serious manner and with concrete suggestions. The representatives were of more than one ethnic origin. The staff response was, in the immediate sense, constructive and understanding. It is over the longer term, however, that these bodies must be evaluated and we would like to see further evidence of their influence.

While School 2 did not appear to have equivalent group sessions there was some similar work in School 3. A group work session was organised by care staff for boys in one House unit which included some from minority ethnic groups. At the outset the boys were asked to display their understanding of the basic rule of confidentiality. The rules were then clarified, with boys reading out written statements. One boy who had difficulty in reading but eventually succeeded was commended by staff.

A counselling question was put to the boys about what angered or frustrated them. They mentioned being accused unjustly and not sleeping. One boy referred to reading as frustrating. In discussion, most of the boys were responsive and active, giving jocular as well as serious answers. But others were more restless and less forthcoming and one in particular who said nothing in the session, confided to the researcher, 'Isn't it boring?'. Suggestions for ways of dealing with frustrations and problems were requested by staff. When a boy suggested having closed circuit television in bedrooms, there was general laughter accompanied by imitations of masturbation. The staff response was an approving, 'Well, you are growing boys'. There was a more serious discussion about dealing with bullying and sleeplessness, during which staff asked questions and gave advice.

The counselling therefore addressed the emotional aspect of behaviour in a group setting and how problems could be resolved. It dealt appropriately with the rules for confidential counselling, allowed young people to set an agenda and facilitated the giving of advice. The session was conducted in a positive and warm atmosphere that acknowledged the humour of adolescent boys. However, it was more successful with one half of the group and clearly 'turned off' one member. There was no evidence that children from minority ethnic groups were less than full participants.

Positive peer culture (PPC) at School 4 was the most ambitious and systematic attempt in any of the schools to harness the power of the group to change behaviour. From a limited base initially, group sessions in the different houses built progressively on these principles. Children in the three lower houses filed into their house lounges after lunch every day and were led through a group session by one of the house staff. Sessions were long, up to three-quarters of an hour, for example. Children rapidly settled and were generally occupied but signs of restlessness, tension and conflict among them tended to emerge. Children were asked to report their experiences in the previous 24 hours. In more advanced sessions, an individual child became the focus of the meeting and children were asked in turn how they would help him or her to achieve a goal, such as avoiding a sanction. Some of the children were reproved by the leaders for lapsing into PPC jargon which signified ritual obeisance rather than sincerity.

A child who failed to specify the support she had given to the child who was the focus suffered the loss of a point on one occasion. Here the behavioural regime and positive peer culture came into collision. Nonetheless praise was given on this occasion both to the child in focus and some of the other 'supporters'. Minor misbehaviours were sometimes mildly reproved or ignored. On other occasions, even the silent mouthing of an objectionable word was noticed and the child was sanctioned with a 'time out' outside the room. When there was discussion about an unpopular child receiving a punch, the leader encouraged the children to make an admission, warning that, if not, several children might be sanctioned. But no public admission was forthcoming. When children, on the other hand, were reported as having been successful, the sessions gave several opportunities to leaders to offer praise to individuals. In addition, praise was very much set forth as a model behaviour for children supporting their peers and reported instances of it appeared almost like a currency that could be cashed at the PPC session. Warnings to peers were also encouraged. The structures of the session gave opportunities to girls and boys to make contributions. One case was cited of a girl who had, in time, overcome her reluctance to speak; another used a session to complain about a boy's unwanted attention.

The agenda for PPC-type sessions was usually highly specific and individualised but centred on school experience. Clearly, relationships and conflicts within the groups were aired but these were not necessarily resolved and leaders were aware of the ways in which children's responses could become mechanical. The structure of school discipline and in particular its behavioural systems was very much present throughout.

Control

The schools were not secure accommodation for children and under present legislation are not allowed to be. It was common practice in the schools to lock external doors only at night. This gave some leeway for hiding on the premises or absconding, examples of which were discovered in each school. What strategies were then in place to deal with the more extreme forms of behaviour?

Controls in School 1 were supported by sanctions based on the withdrawal of privileges. Some of the control problems affected the buildings and general safety, such as fires and fire alarms. Window-smashing was explained by one pupil as a response to measures taken to deal with smoking. In another case roof climbing was explained as part of a personal strategy to be sent home. This was ironic as in fact staff were considering whether such behaviour warranted referral to another placement. At School 1 violence was not seen by staff as a problem among the children themselves. Instead, it was seen as a problem for staff. It was nonetheless claimed that children would support staff when assaults took place. The following incident shows how restraint was used.

A boy was observed to spend his evening activity time bullying two girls. At the end of the session he walked towards the main door which a male teacher barred. The boy said, 'I want to go out', and pushed against the teacher. The teacher held the boy and they struggled. The teacher pushed the boy to the floor where he began to scream and cry. Another care staff member was watching this incident. Later that evening, a female care staff member reported that he was quite 'normal'.

At School 2, both the 'independence' unit and the supervised unit for boys contained some children who were seen as potentially highly delinquent and prone to dangerous behaviour. There was evidence that staff faced a form of peer group delinquency which, significantly, represented a collective answer to individuals' problems. It is this kind of peer-supported behaviour that institutions are hard-pressed to confront and makes some children prime candidates for referral to specialised facilities. One boy in the structured unit always sat at a table near the kitchen hatch and to join his table was said to be a privilege. He was said never to refuse a dare and assumed the responsibility of driving cars taken by the group; another boy made badges calling him the TDA King, a reference to taking and driving away cars. Dealing with the behaviour posed difficulties. He was said to be enthusiastic about the outdoor pursuits organised by the school, despite impediments such as curfews, but this programme with its similarities to traditional Intermediate Treatment was being supplemented by a motor vehicle project organised by the school's 'independence unit' in the apparent absence of any other local initiative.

One staff member was particularly concerned about the influence of high-status delinquents on boys who had no previous recorded offences but had other special needs. One of the younger boys in the unit when making a video in school included a gleeful reference to a burglary committed by another boy. A boy was also heard at lunch explaining how to travel fraudulently by train. Delinquency thus appeared to be a general object of fascination and it may have been through this, rather than direct recruitment for specific delinquent acts, that children were subject to possibly adverse influences.

It was in dealing with rule infractions that School 2 showed its reliance on staff discretion. A major sanction at School 2 was withdrawing the privilege of leaving the site. There was a tariff apparently but the decisions were subject to discretion. When two boys returned at breakfast time after staying out the night, there was an intense discussion between staff and boys about whether they should miss a weekend trip. Staff were to be consulted as well as boys, the absconders were told. A staff vote was held yet it was revealed that senior management had decided from the outset to let the boys go on the trip. Though the incident reveals inconsistencies, this attention to individual circumstances was derived from the school's philosophy and, indeed, in the 'independence unit', no official sanctions were used.

At School 2 some staff conversed about the problem of complying with Children Act guidelines on restraint, which they saw as applicable to the school. Their concern was with potential threats to themselves, rather than to other children. During the research, a member of the domestic staff had to receive extended hospital treatment after warding off a weapon used by one child against another. It is in this context that evidence about restraint at School 2 must be considered.

There were instances in which holding was apparently used to combine care and control. For example, a boy who was said to have been violent to a staff member at the school and who had a long history of absconding from other placements was closely hugged by a female care staff member during an assembly. Similarly, a teacher constantly held the hand of an extremely mischievous boy. This boy presented difficulties in the nurturing unit, which led to a short episode of restraint. On that particular day, he had ripped two shirts and another boy had done the same, apparently in imitation. During the evening he hit the fire alarm and made himself sick on the floor. He was reproved and told to sit on the stairs, but he then moved away. He was told to move back and held tight. He was calmly saying 'Sorry, sorry', as the children were supervised onto a minibus for an evening out.

In such cases it is vital to have an understanding of what has preceded an episode of restraint and how a particular child's difficulties have been interpreted by staff. It would be wrong in these circumstances to underestimate the implication of control in physically holding children.

A more serious incident that occurred in mid-1992 was reported in writing by a male member of the care staff.

> At 9.50 pm... I asked (the boy) to take off his trainers. He refused point blank, so I told him that I would have to take them off him. He moved himself from the office saying that he was leaving the unit. I followed him and prevented him from pushing the front doors open. A struggle then ensued and I restrained the boy who was becoming verbally abusive to me and at one stage actually punched me. I let him up and invited him to hit me, which he didn't. He then calmed considerably and I escorted him to his room. During the restraint other members of staff were present.

In this report the actions of the care staff member were concerned at first with the boy's dress, then with absconding. The reasons for restraint appeared not to be straightforwardly to do with an identifiable danger but with a more complex agenda which included more mundane and less serious concerns.

Various sanctions were permitted at School 3. Restraint was used in situations where children lost their tempers. For example, a boy toyed with his lunch and declined a pudding. He was placed at a small table nearby. As the meal things were cleared up, he went into a tantrum, banging and shouting repeatedly, 'I want my fucking pudding'. Staff steered him away from the table and talked to him. He began to calm down after a few minutes. At lunch the following day the same scenario was repeated and the boy was taken out, held by two staff. In this scuffle a staff member sustained an injury to a finger. The other children looked embarrassed.

Similarly, a report was made by a female care staff member at School 3 about an incident in early 1992 when a girl refused to wash but eventually complied. A chair was thrown at the staff member. The girl then took her tape recorder over to class. The staff member then asked for it because this was not allowed. The report continued:

She refused persistently and I had to remove it from her. I then had to physically take her over to school. (A domestic assistant came with me.) On the way (the child) bit my arm and my hand. I put her outside the office where she continued to scream and shout and be abusive. (A senior staff member) then took (the child) to class and calmed her down.

It is clear that an underlying theme in this incident was a judgment by a staff member about the appropriate use of force to maintain the school rules and the daily routine. Despite the painful violence shown to her, the care staff member here appeared to focus on using her own powers to prepare the child for school. Restraint in School 3 was used to confront a range of situations in which the children's emotions flared.

Control at School 4 had been implemented through token economy fines, time-out and physical means. The school had maintained a policy of using 'time-out' for minor and serious offences until consultation with social services led to its abolition midway through the research. When used, it could be a serious measure. A boy had been placed on time-out for striking a teacher, requiring three stitches. This event had taken place the previous week. It was explained that he had been removed from the school and on his return was kept apart during 'loose periods' for three days. It was suggested that other children felt vengefully towards him. He sat on a chair in the main hall, facing the wall, and leaning his head against it. His meals were eaten at a separate table. The researcher was told that generally the boy's father was 'supportive' and that he felt he could now converse positively with his son.

But time-out was also used for a range of disapproved actions. A mere sign of distracted behaviour could lead to a lesser time-out. During a group session modelled on positive peer culture, two girls began to laugh. They were accompanied from the room by staff. The words 'Kiss my arse' were heard from a girl in the corridor. One returned, but the other was discovered half an hour later on a chair outside the room. Time-out was applied to absconders on their return and lasted for about an hour, by which time children were said to have composed themselves. Such periods contrast with the five to 10 minutes recommended in the literature (Yule, 1978). Children in the two upper houses were not subjected to time-out.

In School 4, as we have seen, there was a clear written policy on the use of physical force to ensure children complied with reasonable requests to take actions specified by staff. It was therefore expected that incidents of this type would be reported, such as the following which took place in 1991.

A boy refused to go and see a female teacher on the playground. A male teacher repeated the request three or four times.

I gave him one chance, he still refused so I grabbed his coat and forced him towards the wall and (the female teacher). He continued to refuse so I took him forcefully to (the Deputy Head)'s office.

An undated report described in detail how a boy was sanctioned for reasons left unspecified. He was set to work in the grounds but stopped.

(A staff member) went over, took his hands, placed them on the broom, his on top, and made him sweep. The boy flinched, groaned, stating, "I can do it".

Such practices were referred to among children as 'the bounce' and were the subject of policy changes during the research, influenced by the Children Act guidance (Department of Health, 1991, p15). As at other schools, a perception of the potential for violent conflict with staff ran beneath the surface. A senior staff member candidly spoke of the element of fear preventing assaults on staff, though, as the serious incident described previously shows, assault on staff was still a risk.

Living together

It was clear that group living was conducted in characteristic ways in the different schools. But what stands out is the impression that, with some exceptions, group situations were not handled in a way that suggested highly specialist techniques. Rather, the task of group care was often to do with implementing quite ordinary decisions within an admittedly specialised framework. For the most part, on a day to day basis, care staff seemed concerned with acting in what appeared to be natural and commonsense ways when dealing with demanding children. There were, however, examples of more strategic approaches – the School Council in School 1, the independence curriculum in School 2, and the group counselling in School 3. In School 4, positive peer culture sessions, behavioural systems and time-out created more pervasive influences on group care tasks. In contrast, School 2's therapeutic interventions were often individualised.

Each school had developed a range of sanctions to deal with misbehaviour, but there were occasions when staff judged that physical restraint was necessary. Occasions were identified in each school where the circumstances included children's attempts to move out of a supervised area or to refuse compliance with the routine. In these cases there is room for doubt about the extent to which these actions were in keeping with the spirit of the guidance and regulations issued under the Children Act 1989, which made clear that harm to the child, other children or property were the only proper criteria for restraint to be used (Department of Health, 1991 and 1993). The experience of policy changes at School 4 tends to confirm this point. A clear interdisciplinary lead will be necessary in future, especially in view of the fact that as recently as 1989 the issue of physical restraint did not feature significantly in a HMI report (HMI, 1989).

Summary

- Observations of lessons showed that curriculum objectives varied from school to school, with different emphases on the relevance of GCSE.
- Classes were organised so as to focus pupils' attention on their individual tasks.
- Teachers' behaviour showed qualities of patience and helpfulness to individuals, but praise for pupils' work and behaviour was not as frequent as might have been expected.
- There was no significant evidence to show that girls were adversely treated in the classroom.
- There were a very few instances when children from minority ethnic groups were observed to suffer from adverse treatment in an educational setting.
- The design of living arrangements reflected to some extent the diversity of philosophies among schools, varying from separately structured and located units to a planned, progressive hierarchy of houses.
- A lack of accommodation resources was identified at School 3.
- Group activities outside the classroom were sometimes clearly designed to fulfil educational aims, but in other cases this was less clear-cut.
- It was not easy to discern unusual or specialised techniques in staff's handling of group situations, though the structure of children's daily experience showed the imprint of the schools' various philosophies.
- Various forms of group work, developing personal and social skills, were observed, including a School Council and sessions influenced by Positive Peer Culture.
- The use of physical restraint, in terms fully consistent with the Children Act 1989 guidance, appeared to be a difficult issue for all the schools.

5. The assessment of progress

What is 'progress'?

The idea of progress in dealing with difficult behaviour was closely associated at one time with the concepts of pathology which dominated thinking about children's problems until quite recently (Balbernie, 1966). According to this medical model the location of a problem within the child meant that something therapeutic applied to that child would lead to an amelioration or even 'cure'. Hence the notion of progress was central to any consideration of the effects of provision, because it corresponded with strong therapeutic intentions. The accent of the medical model was only shifted slightly by the spread of behavioural ideas which rejected the search for malfunctions inside the child in favour of a concern with observable processes of behaviour. Progress itself was still at the heart of behavioural thinking which looked only to more effective and efficient methods of changing the problem behaviour. The idea of therapeutic progress lived on.

We have to be careful to distinguish this particular version of progress from other ways of evaluating the effect of provision, which may reveal other intentions such as giving opportunity, nurturance, respite or shelter to children. These are apparently less ambitious aims which presuppose that children possess a variety of needs and wants and are not simply repositories of problems. Nonetheless, the fulfilment of such aims requires no less thought and effort; it implies that a whole range of issues associated with a 'normal' childhood can be appropriately addressed in a way that takes full account of 'difficult' children's 'abnormal' or marginal situation. The aim is not to produce 'cured' individuals but individuals capable of functioning in their social settings. Progress in these terms means that young people are enabled to achieve both educational and social goals. It means too that certain important links, with parents and the home community, for example, are not broken. The maintenance of good health and the protection of children from harm are also part of this promotion of general developmental goals. Children's sense of identity requires active support. As they grow up they need to take increasing responsibility for looking after themselves and for controlling their own behaviour.

To obtain a comprehensive overview of progress, the recently published

Assessment and Action Records, approved by the Department of Health for use with children being looked after by local authorities, were adapted (Parker and others, 1991). These specified general topics and particular items which represent aspects of development over the medium term, namely, a year. They were designed to be completed by care staff in consultation with the child. The Record specifically designed for children aged ten years to 15 years was selected for use in this study. Despite the fact that the average age proved to be on the high side, namely 15 years of age, the Record appeared appropriate for this group of children mainly of secondary school age, of which a proportion had learning difficulties.

The Record was developed to tap the knowledge of those most closely concerned with an individual case. While some of the questions asked for a simple factual response, most required the selection of a point on a simple scale. The reasons for this approach are discussed in Parker and others (1991). One benefit is that they do not require specialist knowledge to complete and interpret. Because the response calls upon a subjective judgement the results may not be comparable among individual children.

In order to add a new dimension to the approach in the Record, and to strengthen its validity as a research tool, it was decided to ask a series of up to four individual staff to complete separately important sections of the standard questionnaire about each case. Here it was the degree of agreement about the cases that was seen as vital. In addition it was felt to be important to interview the children separately and individually using the same basic questions. Parents were also sent a shorter questionnaire covering similar ground. A cluster of assessments was therefore produced about each case.

It was not possible, because of the relatively brief duration of this research, to repeat this exercise after a sufficient period of time, so as to enable comparison of two actual assessments. Because 'difficult' children do not settle easily after admission, it would have been necessary to collect data year on year (Roe, 1965; Millham and others, 1978). We did not have a year to wait for the second round of results. Instead, it was decided to formulate many items in the form of, firstly, a broad question about the situation a year ago, and, secondly, a follow-up question about the present, which was scaled to show whether progress was perceived. Some topics were, on the other hand, approached with data at admission as the implicit starting point. Thus, the items on 'EBD' were set in the present and were analysed in relation to data recorded at admission. In order to handle the number of items necessary for a specialised group in a residential education setting, and to include educational data, the questions required some adaptation and addition. Since the data were, in many cases, retrospective judgements, they are properly understood as evaluations from the perspective of the **present**, rather than from **both** the past and the present. They resemble the results of customer satisfaction surveys, where the suppliers of a service are also asked to give their views on its effectiveness. In this case, the child and the parents were customers and the staff the suppliers. This is very different from an impersonal evaluation by an outsider. Where possible, of course, objective measures were added to the data set. But it is difficult to envisage how externally standardised measures could have addressed so directly the views of such diverse assessors on the self-same topics. In addition, the Record enjoyed two advantages: it was certainly comprehensive and it was likely to generate a wealth of comparable data as it became used in local authority settings.

In practice, the researcher administered questionnaires to all the children individually while the staff completed written questionnaires. Prior to the child interview, the majority of the children had taken part in an exploratory small group interview and had responded to semi-structured questions. The purposes and guidelines of the research had been explained beforehand and an individual letter of introduction had been given to the children at the outset.

It is important to recognise that interview data do not emerge from an impersonal instrument, like a test tube. In fact, their validity depends partly on the language used in questions and also, and more significantly, on the relationship between the researcher and the subjects. In studies such as this it is vital to try to establish a relationship in which the subjects find the questions interesting and indeed feel their participation is welcomed and appreciated. Researchers must spend time introducing themselves and making themselves a routine and unobtrusive part of the everyday living situation. In so far as they can, they must make themselves available to vulnerable and sometimes distressed children. Indeed, in three of the schools six children took the opportunity in private to report to the researcher specific matters of serious concern that were discussed later with the Heads. These included allegations of abuse at home, as well as sexual exploitation by pupils, violence by staff, victimisation and suicidal thoughts while at school. As the previous chapter showed, a considerable amount of time was spent in ordinary contact with the children who were later interviewed. It was in fact a teacher at one school who pointed out that the validity of the data depended on the relationship built up between the researcher and the children. A considerable investment of this type was required before a satisfactory interview could be even contemplated.

Children's ages

At admission to the four schools, the 67 children in the sample were on average 12-years-old. At follow-up by this study, on average, two years eight months had elapsed since the time of admission.

Table 5.1   Ages of children at admission and at follow-up

	1. Admission	2. Follow-up
Mean	12-years-old	15-years-old
Range	8-15 years	10-17 years

The findings emphasise how many of the initially stable placements had endured. A large proportion of those who had lasted a year in placement had in fact stayed for well over a year. The placement in a residential EBD school was for these children their major form of education at the secondary stage. Clearly, residential special education was a very significant part of their general schooling. At the same time it follows that the children's reviews had not contradicted the appropriateness of placements. If so the comments from the schools about weaknesses in the reviewing system must lead to some concern about the monitoring of such long-lasting placements. It should also be recalled from chapter 3 that other children placed in school during the same period had already left, sometimes through transfer, sometimes through unplanned departure. This report of progress, therefore, applies to initially stable placements, not necessarily to all those admitted to residential EBD provision.

Family circumstances and relationships

Data was first of all collected from care staff on the frequency of home visits by children. Schools varied in offering 52 or 38-week placements. For example, no 52-week placements were available at School 3. In fact, 80-85 per cent of all cases in the four schools spent the three holiday periods at home. This still left three children in school at Christmas and four during the Easter and Summer vacations. There was a large variation in the proportions visiting home at weekends during term time (Berridge, 1985). It emerged that 18 per cent of cases visited home on only two weekends out of ten during the school year. Indeed, 34 per cent of cases visited home fortnightly or less often. On the other hand, 43 per cent of the sample made such visits on at least nine weekends in ten. The variations among cases suggest that placements cannot be assumed to involve a standard period of time at school. For a few children a holiday was spent in school; for many, weekend visits were limited. The complexity of these arrangements made it all the more necessary to explore children's perceptions of home.

Feelings about 'home' were explored in a series of questions to pupils. It was not specified what form of home the child had in mind, which in some cases might have been a children's home. A year ago, 76 per cent felt they had missed being at home when they were in school. Currently, 56 per cent missed home 'a lot', or 'a bit'. Last year 63 per cent reported that they got on well with the people who looked after them, 67 per cent now got on better and 10 per cent worse. Fifty eight per cent preferred to live at home all the time. A substantial proportion, indeed a majority, favoured their home rather than a residential placement, and relationships in the home setting were mostly felt to be satisfactory and improving.

Care staff similarly reported 72 per cent of children missing home a year ago and 43 per cent currently. A year ago 60 per cent related well to the people who looked after them and 39 per cent showed an improvement currently and 15 per cent a deterioration. Forty-nine per cent would prefer to live at home all the time, according to care staff. The views of care staff and children tended to correspond, though care staff underestimated the proportion preferring to live permanently at home and were less confident about improvement in relationships. Data specifically about parental contacts and relationships point in a similar direction.

Removal to a placement far from home represents a challenge to relationships within the family which, in many cases, were stressful at admission. It would be a serious shortcoming if residential education were to lead to poorer relationships at home. However, many children reported no deterioration in contact or quality of relationship.

Table 5.2   Stable or improved relations with parents (children's view)

	Contact		Relationship quality	
	No	%	No	%
With mothers	38	56	51	76
With fathers	27	40	44	66

Despite these majority findings, we should not overlook the six children in the sample of 67 whose relationship with their mothers deteriorated and the eight children whose relationship with their fathers suffered in the previous year. A large number of children – 37 – were not in continuous contact with their fathers. It is interesting to note that the results for 'relationship quality' exceeded the figures for 'contact'. For some children clearly, reduced contact did not necessarily lead to a deterioration in relationship quality – an important distinction. We now turn to the care staff.

Table 5.3   Stable or improved relations with parents (care staff's view)

	Contact		Relationship quality	
	No	%	No	%
With mothers	43	64	44	66
With fathers	27	40	24	36

For the contact dimension, care staff agreed remarkably well with the children. On relationship quality, however, there were fewer responses – 49 in the case of mothers, and only 32 in the case of fathers (or almost half the sample). Presumably, care staff were more often reluctant to assess the quality of relationships. Nonetheless, there was agreement with the children on the small number of deteriorated relationships (five with mothers and eight with fathers). It would seem that care staff were more aware of family contact and of deterioration in relationships than of children's views about relationships more broadly. This finding may have implications for how family relationships were assessed.

There were significant differences among schools for contact with mothers and for fathers (p<.05 and <.01, respectively). Contact with both parents was less frequently positive at School 2 (where there were more children with care experience at admission). The picture elsewhere was more mixed but School 1 achieved second ranking on contact with both parents.

Parental views about contact and relationships added to the picture significantly. All parent respondents had visited the school in the past year but 51 per cent would wish to visit more often. Interestingly, 46 per cent reported a staff visit to their home and 37 per cent wished for more home visits. Fortunately, 66 per cent described telephoning the child as easy, compared with 17 per cent who found it difficult.

A year ago, 83 per cent of parents reported seeing their children 'often' and in 46 per cent of cases this contact had improved, while in ten per cent it had deteriorated. Forty-nine per cent of parents reported that a year ago their children were getting on well with them; in 51 per cent of cases the relationship had improved while there was deterioration in seven per cent.

The response rate for the parental questionnaire was 61 per cent so we must be reasonably cautious in our conclusions. It seems that many in this group showed positive signs of willingness to take an interest in children's schooling and to maintain contact with them. Though there were still signs of strained relationships in about half the cases, there were more perceptions of improvement than of deterioration. The proportions showing change in relationship quality bear comparison with the perceptions of children and staff.

In order to discover the impact of a placement on social contact and friendship, questions were asked about friendships outside school and about any feelings of loneliness when at home. An encouraging 75 per cent of children reported they had at least three good friends outside school but 22 per cent had just one or two friends, or none at all. Thirty-one per cent had felt lonely a year ago when at home and 19 per cent currently felt more lonely than previously. Only 18 per cent were in a youth club or organisation at home. A significant minority therefore reported experiences of loneliness and few friendships. Staff were, however, less aware of numbers of friends than of problems of loneliness. Though they had information about only 76 per cent of cases, they identified 48 per cent of all cases as having one or two friends, or none at all. A year ago, 28 per cent had been lonely at home and 16 per cent were, currently, more lonely. Staff judged that 13 per cent of cases were in a youth club or organisation, largely agreeing with the proportion identified by children.

Children placed away from home and defined as difficult are likely to carry a burden of insecurity because of their treatment. To what extent did the children feel supported? Eighty-three per cent said they were called by their proper name at school. Yet only 49 per cent said they knew all or most of the reasons for the residential placement. In the past year, someone (not specified) had talked to 54 per cent about the story of their life. Seventy-nine per cent were now being told that they were doing 'fairly well' or 'very well' at school. Seventy-three per cent thought they were good at doing 'quite a lot of things' or 'a great many things'. Care staff differed in feeling that 76 per cent knew all or most of the reasons for placement. However, only 12 per cent of staff reported life story work. Children appeared to have reported general conversations about their past rather than specific occasions of counselling. Interestingly, staff were slightly less positive about children's confidence in being able to do things, identifying it in 61 per cent of cases.

A combined measure of perceived identity support was computed, adding together the use of proper names, knowing reasons for placement, experience of praise and discussion of life story. For these four items the mean score was 2.73, 10 per cent scoring only one and 19 per cent scoring a maximum of four. Care staff's perspective was similar, with an average score of 2.59 but with fewer at the top end – nine per cent scoring one and the same proportion scoring the maximum. Despite the schools' different approaches, there were no significant differences in outcome on these measures.

How then did the children perceive their school experience? They were asked whether they were treated fairly, to which 55 per cent replied positively. Only 7 per cent considered themselves treated unfairly. Children from minority ethnic groups were more likely to hold a positive view ($p=0.05$). Given their minority presence in the schools this was a satisfying result. There was also some difference amongst children in the different schools but this did not reach statistical significance. In addition, children were asked to rate their mood on the first day of a new term (Smith and Tomlinson, 1989). Forty per cent gave a positive opinion compared with a less enthusiastic 60 per cent. Asked about a placement in a comprehensive school, 42 per cent felt they would learn more while 37 per cent thought they would learn less. While most children considered they received fair treatment, there were therefore mixed views about the benefits of a residential school. On the other hand, parents in the survey were more enthusiastic, 83 per cent endorsing the schools' fairness and 85 per cent describing them as 'good'. Eighty-eight per cent of parents also considered the schools explained things well, while 73 per cent wanted the children to remain at their schools.

Another effect of placement is to draw children away from their home communities for periods of time. It was found that children from minority ethnic groups were significantly less likely to report stable or continuous contact with other members of their ethnic group ($p<.05$). However, care staff did not report a difference of this magnitude. The findings raise the possibility that such contacts were not being given the attention that research suggests they deserve (Stone, 1983). The Children Act has also given weight to maintaining religious affiliations. According to children, 45 per cent had visited a place of worship at home in the past year compared with only 19 per cent reported by care staff. Given the centrality of religion and ethnic origin as elements of children's lives, it is vital that these issues are given the most careful attention in the future.

Abuse

A further significant aspect of children's experience was the incidence of abuse and bullying in the past year and, in particular, what information about it was held by staff. Abuse was a significant experience prior to admission. How many had suffered in the past year? Staff reported that four per cent had definitely suffered from physical abuse and six per cent from sexual abuse. However, 21 per cent in all were reported to have experienced some form of suspected or confirmed abuse; 13 per cent had experienced suspected or confirmed physical abuse and 13 per cent similarly sexual abuse and six per cent both forms of suspected or confirmed abuse. Data was not gathered from staff about who was responsible or where the abuse had taken place.

Was this experience confined, however, to those cases specifically placed by social services in which abuse might have been a factor in referral and hence more predictable? Of the 14 reported cases, 11 placements had been paid for by LEAs and only two by social services. (There was uncertainty surrounding the remaining case.) It appears that abuse was certainly not confined to the minority of cases for which social services had taken a major responsibility. A minority of abused children were therefore found in establishments which appeared to lie outside the full scope of the Children's Homes Regulations and Guidance.

In addition, severe bullying in the past year was confirmed in four per cent of cases and suspected in 11 per cent. There were significant differences among schools in the reported prevalence of physical abuse and also of severe bullying in the past year (p<.01 and <.05). School 3 had a consistently higher ranking for both. However, no significant differences in victimisation rates amongst boys or girls or ethnic groups could be found. For a proportion of children, admission to a residential school did not mean that they were fully protected from abusive experiences. Clearly the system of management and inspection of such schools needs to reflect this unfortunate reality.

Health and well-being

No fewer than 87 per cent of children said their health last year had been good; for 52 per cent it was now better, but for 18 per cent it was worse. Children were asked a series of questions about their health including their health behaviour. In addition to the general question above, they included questions about progress in dealing with any embarrassing conditions, in eating fresh fruit and vegetables, taking part in swimming and sport, not smoking and not drinking alcohol. Their responses were amalgamated into a general measure of health progress. It emerged that 73 per cent reported progress in up to half of the eight items, compared with 27 per cent reporting progress in over half. The mean was a progression on 3.48 items. This compared with a mean of only 0.6 items reported by care staff – a substantial difference. Care staff also reported that 82 per cent had received education about contraception and AIDS, but fewer children had received this help at Schools 2 and 3 (p<.05).

Forty-six per cent of children had suffered at least one minor illness over the previous year, while the results for the whole sample ranged from one to three illnesses. Children at School 4 were more frequently reported as having minor illnesses but clearly the lowest was School 2 (p<.05). Girls were reported to suffer from more illnesses than boys: while the mean for boys was 0.5, for girls it was 1.3, corresponding to a significant difference (p<.05).

Health impairments were also identified in many cases: 42 per cent possessed at least one, while the results for the whole sample also ranged from one to three. This was a marked increase over the rate recorded at admission. The three children from minority ethnic groups experiencing impairments were found to suffer from more impairments than others with similar difficulties (p<.05).

Children were also asked their opinion of their medical care. Seventy-nine per cent said that a year ago it had been good, 31 per cent said it had since improved and 15 per cent that it had deteriorated. The view of parents was also sought: 88 per cent felt that the children's health care had been good a year ago, 24 per cent said it had since improved and only one reported deterioration.

Care staff reported a mean of 2.2 medical examinations in the last year. Though 72 per cent of children received at least one examination, 3 per cent received none and information on 25 per cent was not available. Of the whole sample, 54 per cent received at least two dental examinations, but 30 per cent received none or only one. Information on 16 per cent was again not available. The number of reports of examinations significantly differed among the schools with School 4 the highest and School 3 the lowest for both medical and dental examinations (p<.01 and <.01, respectively). School 3 was, however, the only one to report overnight stays in hospital, for four cases. We were informed that 33 per cent had been immunised for BCG and the same proportion for rubella. Fifteen per cent of children wore glasses, six per cent a brace and one child a hearing aid.

Emotional and behavioural difficulties

The emotional and behavioural difficulties of children were studied by asking the child and four staff to rate each of 15 items on a scale to show the presence or absence of a current problem relating to that child. The results are set out the table on page 107. We can look, first of all, at the problems most frequently identified. The results show that children most frequently rated nail biting as a problem (67 per cent of the whole sample) followed by frequent swearing and making trouble in class (45 and 40 per cent). What was the ranking of problems by the staff as a group? All staff in effect agreed that frequent swearing was the most prevalent problem. Lack of compliance in the home was agreed by all staff but the teachers to be the second most prevalent. Lack of concentration was considered third in prevalence by the other staff members but the teachers ranked it second.

Let us now move below the 'top three' problems, as seen by children and staff. Children's responses put lack of concentration fourth in the ranking of prevalence. For care staff, nail biting came in fourth place but, for the deputy heads (care), this position was unexpectedly held by sexual exploitation (taking advantage of a partner). Extreme shyness was perceived by teachers as fourth, while for deputy heads of education, children missing lessons occupied this place. While there were some disagreements between children and staff over the top three rankings, it is clear that further disagreements among staff reflected some specialisation of tasks, with the deputy heads aware of more challenging problems.

Poor sleeping ranked fifth for children, equal with missing lessons, but no staff member ranked it higher than tenth. There was a very high positive and significant correlation between poor sleeping identified at admission and poor sleeping identified by the children during the survey ($r=0.87$). There was no such correlation between the views of staff and children. This suggests continuing problems for a small number of children (7 per cent of the sample) which clearly required attention.

Non-compliance in school ranked fifth for care staff and deputy heads of education, but this position was held for teachers by non-compliance at home and, for deputy heads of care, by nail biting.

If we look at dangerous behaviour, solvent abuse was alleged in a maximum of nine per cent of cases (by care staff) but children and teachers both put it as low as three per cent. Again, alcohol abuse was alleged in a maximum of 24 per cent of cases (by care staff) but teachers perceived it in six per cent, slightly lower than children. In the case of frequent trouble with the law, the maximum was 18 per cent of the sample, claimed by children, while care staff put the proportion as low as seven per cent. None of these behaviours affected a majority of the sample.

Behaviour in school and home presented a more complicated picture. There was some agreement between care staff and deputy heads of care about the proportion of children uncooperative at home, as there was between teachers and deputy heads of education about trouble-making in class and non-compliance in schools. But more children spoke about

Table 5.4 Multiple assessments of emotional and behavioural difficulties

		Eating poorly	Sleeping poorly	Taci-turnity	Extreme shyness	Lack of con-centration	Not compliant at home	Not compliant in school	Frequent swearing	Alcohol abuse	Nail biting	Makes trouble in class	Misses lessons if possible	Frequent law breaking	Sexual exploi-tation	Solvent abuse
Child		11	16	12	11	20	11	8	30	5	45	27	16	12	9	2
	%	17.0	24.6	18.5	16.9	30.8	16.9	12.5	46.9	7.9	67.2	41.5	25.0	18.8	14.5	3.1
	rank	7=	5=	6=	7=	4	7=	9	2	10	1	3	5=	6=	8	11
Care staff Member		13	11	11	14	22	31	17	39	16	20	10	12	5	12	6
	%	19.7	16.6	16.7	21.2	33.9	49.2	26.5	59.1	24.6	29.9	15.4	18.8	7.7	19.0	9.2
	rank	8	10=	10=	7	3	2	5	1	6	4	11	9=	13	9=	12
Deputy Head (Care)		12	4	7	13	24	28	10	32	9	14	9	8	9	17	4
	%	17.9	6.0	10.5	19.4	35.9	41.8	14.9	47.7	13.7	20.9	13.4	12.3	13.5	26.1	6.0
	rank	7	12=	11	6	3	2	8	1	9=	5	9=	10	9=	4	12=
Teacher		2	3	7	20	26	16	23	29	4	10	14	10	6	8	2
	%	3.2	5.1	10.9	31.3	40.0	27.1	34.9	43.9	7.0	14.9	21.5	15.9	9.8	14.1	3.7
	rank	13=	12	9	4	2	5	3	1	11	7=	6	7=	10	8	13=
Deputy Head (teaching)		8	4	12	13	21	23	18	37	10	16	14	19	9	11	5
	%	12.3	6.1	18.2	19.7	31.8	35.9	27.7	56.9	15.4	23.9	21.2	29.2	13.8	16.9	7.7
	rank	13	15	9	8	3	2	5	1	11	6	7	4	12	10	14
Recorded at Admission		-	5	2	1	36	49	57	13	2	-	48	18	6	4	2
	%	-	7	3	1	54	73	85	19	3	-	72	27	9	6	3
	rank	-	8	10=	11	4	2	1	6	10=	-	3	5	7	9	10=

In this table, (%) refers to the proportion of actual responses, excluding missing values.

trouble-making in class and less about non-compliance in the home and school than staff perceptions would have predicted. Indeed the apparent discrepancy between children's self-ratings for non-compliance in school and trouble making in class deserves further investigation. Adults consistently ranked non-compliance in school above trouble-making in class – a plausible comparison – but with children there was a marked reversal of these items. However, there was a correspondence between teachers' ratings of non-compliance in school and children's rating of trouble-making in class, the latter standing at 40 per cent of the sample. This was the reported upper limit for school behaviour problems and may serve as a marker for the purpose of establishing whether or not progress on these issues had occurred since admission.

The analysis of ratings by children and staff was not entirely straightforward. But it was possible to attempt an analysis of progress since admission by comparing ratings made by the researcher from the documents relating to admission. These ratings formed a summary of the documentary information. The ratings included in the table reveal that the most prevalent problem at admission – non-compliance in school – was significantly lower in the current ratings, from 85 per cent to 34 per cent of cases, according to teachers.

Non-compliance at home was noted in 73 per cent of cases at admission; the highest current rating, by care staff, was 46 per cent. Making trouble in class was found in 72 per cent of cases at admission; at follow-up it was rated in a maximum of 40 per cent of cases, by the children themselves. The fourth most prevalent problem at admission was lack of concentration, affecting 54 per cent, compared with a maximum of 39 per cent at follow-up. Missing lessons (including truancy) was recorded in 27 per cent of cases at admission, compared with a maximum of 28 per cent at follow-up. A major difference was evident for the three most prevalent problems at admission, a smaller difference for the fourth, and no difference at all for the fifth.

We need to be clear about what this means. The researcher made notes on the record at admission before studying the survey results. As we have seen, some differences emerged between the information on the record and the consensus of reports available from the survey – on average, over 2 years later. This is not to say that the records told the whole story, nor that the current ratings were infallible. Indeed, there were certain disagreements among the people making the ratings. But the range of ratings suggests that some conclusions can be drawn about the direction of those differences, which broadly indicates some reduction of problems. It should also be noted that 43 per cent of parents felt that children's compliance at home and general behaviour had improved over the past year.

Other items, however, were not so encouraging. Sexual exploitation (taking advantage of a partner) was recorded in six per cent of cases at admission, but found in a maximum of 25 per cent of cases, by deputy heads (care). In a coeducational setting, such behaviour calls for close attention. Swearing, alcohol abuse, eating problems, poor sleeping, shyness and nail biting were more prevalent than the earlier records would have suggested. It could be argued that sexuality and alcohol use were more relevant to 15-year-olds than to 12-year-olds. However, the other items point to areas of concern that were not frequently recorded at admission for reasons that need exploration. It appeared that the records tended to focus on problems posed by the child for others rather than on problems personally experienced. The need to record personal problems more systematically becomes apparent.

Another way of looking at this evidence is to examine the distribution of problems among children. In other words, how **many** problems were attributed to individuals?

Table 5.5   Number of emotional and behavioural difficulties at follow-up

	Children	Care Staff	Deputy Head (Care)	Teacher	Deputy Head (Education)
Mean	3.61	3.62	2.99	2.73	3.33
Std. Dev.	2.41	2.43	2.51	2.22	2.67
Range	0-10	0-12	0-12	0-9	0-12

The comparison of accumulated scores reveals that, on average, children were normally reported to display at least three problems but their scores tended to range from zero to 12 out of a possible maximum of 15. In fact ten per cent of children rated themselves as showing no problems, while care staff similarly rated nine per cent and teachers 16 per cent. Presumably, questions might be asked about the reason for these children's continued attendance at EBD schools. One child admitted, in effect, to ten problems while care staff rated one as showing 12 problems. Teachers considered that two children showed nine problems. There appeared to be no marked difference among the average scores. Children were just as forthcoming as staff – if not more so – about the number of problems they described. Teachers gave the lowest average assessment and care staff the highest, the latter very close to that of children.

There were few significant differences among sections of the sample in the number of problems reported. However, care staff, the deputy head (care) and teachers at School 2 all gave higher scores than elsewhere (p<.05; <.05; <.05). The children's own scores at this school were also higher than elsewhere but not to a statistically significant degree. The extent of problems at School 2 is a theme that also emerges from a study of further data on offending.

Before this is examined, a further level of analysis needs to be explored. The responses to questions about emotional and behavioural difficulties evidently require careful interpretation. In order to clarify their meaning further, it was possible to compare the responses of children and staff as well as those of different staff members about as many individual cases as possible. This was done using statistical correlation techniques. The results confirmed that there were more significant positive correlations among the responses of staff members than between the children and the staff: 71 out of a possible 90 correlations among staff compared with only 20 out of a possible 60 between the child and the staff. Thus, staff tended to agree among themselves more often than they did with children. The level of the correlation for the items was also higher among staff than between staff and children (range 0.21 – 0.87 and mode 0.4 among staff, compared with range 0.22 – 0.54 and mode 0.3, between children and staff). The most frequent correlations between children's and staff's responses were for frequent trouble with the law, trouble making in class, missing lessons and alcohol abuse; no significant correlations were found for nail biting, reluctance to talk, non-compliance at home, swearing, sexual exploitation and, as we saw earlier, sleeping problems. It seems that more visible threats to the social order of the school were the subject of greater agreement than were other items.

It is therefore necessary to be cautious about drawing precise conclusions about individual cases as distinct from groups of cases. It is nonetheless worthwhile to concentrate on the set of group findings, based on different perspectives, because, taken together, these make possible a general overview of any particular outcome.

Offending, absconding and exclusion

A discouraging trend in offending seemed to emerge from the rating for those frequently in trouble with the law. While nine per cent fell into this category at admission, 18 per cent put themselves in that category at follow-up. It should be remembered that 15 years of age has been the peak age for offending. In order for this information to be placed in context, data was sought on the number of children with a record of offences known to care staff, which is shown in the following table.

Table 5.6 Children committing offences by type and number of offences

Type of offence	Number of offences					
	1	2	3	4	5	Total children
Theft	3	1	2	0	0	6
Taking vehicle without consent	2	0	0	0	0	2
Burglary	2	0	0	0	0	2
Assault	2	0	0	0	0	2
Sexual offences	1	0	0	0	0	1
Other offences	1	0	0	0	0	1
All offences	6	1	2	0	1	10

While the upper part of the table indicates how many children committed particular offences (19 offences in total), the bottom line shows that in all there were ten offenders in the previous year (15 per cent of the total). A significant difference among schools was found for this category of 'all offences', with School 2 leading the others (p<.05).

School 2's higher ranking was statistically confirmed by the data for arrests, and for particular offences – taking a vehicle without consent, theft, burglary, sexual offences and 'other offences' (p<.01; <.05; <.05; <.05; <.01; <.01). A minority of children at School 2 was therefore more often responsible for a whole range of offences, including relatively serious matters, compared with children at other schools. No significant differences were found between the total number of offences committed by boys and girls, or ethnic groups.

Data on police contacts did not add anything significantly new to this picture. Six children were reported as having been arrested (one on no fewer than 17 occasions) while six were noted as having been charged. Again, School 2 led the ranking for arrests as well as for placements in police protection, of which there were six in all.

Leaving school without permission is regarded as a cause for concern, if it occurs frequently. One third of the sample had done so at least once in the previous year, absconding on 58 occasions in all. The rate in School 2 was higher than elsewhere, corresponding to a significant difference (p<.05). However, no significant difference was found between boys and girls, nor between those from minority and other ethnic groups. School 2's higher ranking for absconding was paralleled by its ranking for children placed in police protection.

The rate of delinquency and absconding at School 2 should partly be understood in the context of its admissions of offenders (a feature shared by School 4) and children previously controlled inadequately. Its location within an urban area may also have been relevant. The disappointing findings on delinquency echo a long-established conclusion about residential placements (Millham and others, 1978; Cornish and Clarke, 1975).

Only seven children were excluded during the year, two of these on two occasions. The rate of exclusion from school was therefore only 0.14 but with a standard deviation of 0.43, for 63 cases where information was available. The highest rate of exclusion was at School 3 (a mean of 0.28 for 18 cases) followed by School 2 (0.15 for 13 cases). But at School 4, there had been no exclusions in 15 cases – a confirmation of school policy. Nevertheless these small differences were not statistically significant for the schools, boys and girls, or ethnic groupings. Exclusion is clearly a double-edged measure for schools dealing with vulnerable and reputedly difficult children who are considered to require constant supervision. The policy of one school not to exclude raises questions about whether or not exclusion could have been avoided elsewhere.

Personal responsibility and self-care

Problems of behaviour in a narrow sense are not the only concern for people looking after children who live away from their parents. To function acceptably in their social settings, children will be expected to show an increasing capacity to take responsibility for their actions, to take care of themselves, to look presentable and so on. Residential work by its nature contains a risk of maintaining dependence yet it can also be a basis for increasing opportunity and choice not available to children in other settings. The next group of findings deals in turn with self-control, the growth of autonomy and widening of experience, with self-care skills and, finally, social presentation.

To change behaviour is not itself adequate. To change people's awareness that they can alter their behaviour is an important precondition of lasting change. Stealing, solvent abuse and being quiet when necessary were chosen to illustrate this theme. In fact, 75 per cent of children felt that they had some ability to reject an opportunity to steal – a finding consistent with our other delinquency data. Indeed, 58 per cent felt they had improved in their ability to control the impulse to steal. By comparison, 48 per cent said they had rejected an opportunity to sniff glue or aerosols and 70 per cent felt their self-control in this respect had improved. A year ago, 79 per cent knew of places where they were expected to be quiet but only 40 per cent said they had improved their ability to be quiet when it was expected of them. The data on progress suggest that stealing and solvent abuse were not major temptations for most of this group, while noisiness was! Such findings tend to confirm the type of challenge that their behaviour presented in most cases. The mean score for the combined variables was 1.69 (Std. Dev. 1.06) compared with a score by care staff (on the same items) of 0.91 (Std. Dev. 0.97). Children therefore saw their self-control developing rather more than did care staff. Analysis showed no differences among sections of the sample on this measure. However, on improved control of solvent abuse and stealing combined, there was a difference in the judgement of deputy heads (care) with School 4 the highest and School 3 the lowest ranked (p < .05).

Personal responsibility extends beyond self-control. It was important to find out about children's experience of being trusted, allowed choices and increasingly going on school outings. Forty-eight per cent of children felt they were trusted to do 'many' or 'several' things; 43 per cent felt they were allowed to choose how they used their time 'quite a lot' or 'a great deal' and 42 per cent were going on more outings compared with a year ago. According to care staff, a greater proportion of children were trusted and given choice (58 and 67 per cent) and a similar proportion were undertaking more outings (37 per cent). The combined average score for the attitudes of children was 1.33 (Std. Dev. 0.96) and for care staff 1.65 (Std. Dev. 0.89). There were significant differences among schools in the children's scores for personal responsibility with School 3 in the highest and School 4 in the lowest rank (p < .05). It appeared therefore that children at School 3 felt they were given more responsibility compared with those at School 4.

If functioning in society is seen as an important criterion of progress, the capacity of children to look after themselves must be monitored. In residential placements, there is sometimes a risk that well-intentioned adult caring may take over and delay the development of important self-care skills. Questions were therefore asked about the child's ability to clean a room, use a pay phone, buy a pair of shoes, change a plug, work out how to travel safely, give elementary first aid and so on. In all, 15 items were included.

On seven self-care items, the proportions of positive responses were over 90 per cent. The lowest proportions were for artificial respiration, puncture repair and changing a plug. A dismaying 22 per cent could not work out on their own the cost of a dinner in a cafe. More alarmingly, six per cent could not make an emergency phone call unaided.

Table 5.7   Self-care skills : items performed without help

	Child (%)
Clean teeth without being told	92
Make bed	92
Make cooked breakfast	81
Wash up	94
Clean a room	95
Know about poisons in the home	85
Use a pay phone	95
Make emergency phone call	91
Work out cost of dinner in cafe	75
Buy pair of shoes	82
Know Green Cross traffic code	88
Change a plug	73
Repair bicycle puncture	58
Work out how to travel safely	76
Pack a bag for weekend	91
Help someone not breathing	52

Parents' views were generally favourable, 56 per cent believing that a year ago children could have done 'quite a lot' or 'a great many' things to look after themselves, while currently this applied to 78 per cent. In order to put the data in context, however, the separate items were scored and the perceptions of staff and children compared.

Table 5.8   Perceptions of children's self-care skills

	Child	Care staff	Teacher
Mean	13.60	10.31	9.72
Std. Dev.	2.05	3.41	4.45

Possible maximum: 15

Children took a more favourable view of their skills than did staff, according to this data. Such findings highlight the importance of raising the skills of as many children as possible. There was nonetheless agreement among children, care staff and teachers about the relative skills of children in the four schools. The most skilled were at School 1, followed by School 4, School 2 and School 3, according to each group ($p<.01$; $<.01$; $<.01$). As we shall see the extent of self-care skills may have an important bearing on schools' academic outcomes. It was also found that boys had a higher opinion of their self-care skills than girls (p<.05).

Another aspect of functioning in social settings is personal presentation. Here, children were asked whether their clothing was clean and also up-to-date and whether their speech was understood. There were positive replies in 90 and 87 per cent of cases to the first two questions but only 66 per cent felt normally able to make themselves understood. Again, a comparison of scores on these items is shown below, indicating broad agreement.

Table 5.9   Perceptions of social presentation

	Child	Care staff	Teacher
Mean	2.49	2.59	2.58
Std. Dev.	0.69	0.68	0.72

Possible maximum: 3

Care staff identified differences among schools, with School 4 leading Schools 1, 3 and 2 in that order (p<.05). Schools 1 and 4 thus shared the two leading places for both self-care skills and social presentation.

Progress in the curriculum

Most children felt their basic skills had improved over the year (reading 79 per cent; spelling 64 per cent; handwriting 72 per cent). Similarly, 63 per cent of parents felt their children were learning more than a year ago. To put these perceptions in context, data was collected on the results of tests in the current year and a year ago. However, analysing the differences in results proved not to be straightforward. The tests themselves were varied. In addition, many of the children were well beyond the age for which most tests were intended.

Progress in the implementation of National Curriculum assessment had not advanced to the point at which a broad range of data could be collected. In particular, changes in the assessment of mathematics made it impossible to report progress in that subject. Some data did emerge on children's progress in English, albeit mainly in one school.

The data for School 4 in particular helps us to understand how changes in levels of achievement were perceived. The collection of such information is also relevant to the more frequent rate of GCSE entry at School 4.

Table 5.10   Progress in English Attainment Targets (AT) in two schools: a comparison of mean attainment levels

			School 2 (4 cases)	School 4 (18 cases)
English	AT1	Last year	2.25	4.11
	AT1	This year	2.75	5.00
	AT2	Last year	2.25	3.67
	AT2	This year	2.25	4.33
	AT3	Last year	1.75	3.67
	AT3	This year	2.25	4.56
	AT4	Last year	1.50	3.44
	AT4	This year	2.00	4.28
	AT5	Last year	1.50	3.28
	AT5	This year	2.25	3.67
	AT4/5	Last year	2.00*	3.11
	AT4/5	This year	2.00	3.67

* 3 cases

To examine how far the implementation of the National Curriculum had influenced children's education, questions were asked about progress in individual subjects.

Table 5.11   Perceived improvements in National Curriculum subjects

		Child Learning		Teacher Attitudes to work		Teacher Performance	
Improvement in:		No	%	No	%	No	%
No of subjects	0–1	4	6	15	22	10	15
	2–3	13	19	25	37	23	34
	4–5	19	28	13	19	16	24
	6–7	20	30	10	15	15	22
	8–9	11	16	4	6	3	4
	Total	67	100	67	100	67	100
	Mean	5.04		3.39		3.88	
	Std. Dev.	2.17		2.32		2.20	

The table shows that, according to children, 46 per cent improved in half the subjects compared with teachers' assessments of 21 per cent improving similarly in attitude and 26 per cent in performance. Teachers were less inclined to perceive progress than were children. Neither children nor teachers saw this degree of improvement in a clear majority of the sample. The results suggest that generalising improvements over the whole National Curriculum had not been perceived as completely successful. There was a significant difference among schools in children's perceptions of learning improvements in National Curriculum subjects. Here School 4 was followed by Schools 3, 1 and 2 in that order ($p < .05$). Teachers also identified differences in attitudes (ranking in order Schools 4, 3, 2 and 1) and in performance (ranking Schools 3, 4, 2 and 1) ($p < .01$ and $< .01$). Teachers and children in Schools 3 and 4 appeared more positive than in other schools. It would be extremely interesting to explore whether these attitudes were influenced by the behavioural assessments routine in those schools.

One of the advantages of residential education is the possible use of evenings for educational purposes (Cole, 1986). In fact, 67 per cent said they received adult help with school work and 54 per cent did homework sometimes or often, compared with 46 per cent who never did homework. Apart from the effect on school work, it is important to know whether an independent reading habit has been established. Asked whether they read a book of their choice in their free time a year ago, 75 per cent answered in the affirmative. This currently happened more frequently in 51 per cent of cases. According to care staff, 69 per cent were reported to receive help with school work while 66 per cent did homework. A year ago, 55 per cent read a book and, in 43 per cent of cases, this happened more frequently. The proportions of busy readers reported by care staff were thus more modest! Responses for homework and adult help were combined into measures of academic focus and support. Children's scores averaged 1.21, compared with 1.36 given by care staff. Both these measures varied among the schools, with School 4 leading School 1 and the others ($p < .01$ and $< .01$). These two leading schools were also ranked highly for self-care skills and social presentation. It may be that there was in effect a 'trade-off' between the academic and these other staff pre-occupations, which was also reflected in curriculum outcomes. Girls also said they received greater academic focus and support ($p = 0.05$).

Educational achievement

There has been a considerable pressure to upgrade educational results in special schools, reflected in the inclusion of special schools in the national league tables of examination results. Alongside this particular development there has been a trend towards associating achievement with certificates of all kinds. It was important to find out how far these developments were reflected among the sample. A table of entries for examinations and certificates is set out below, including not only GCSE but also those associated with the Business and Technology Education Council (BTEC), the City and Guilds of London Institute (CGLI) and the Royal Society of Arts Examinations Board (RSA).

Table 5.12   Entries for examinations and certificates per pupil

No of cases (in brackets)		School	School 1	School 2	School 3	School 4	All cases
(16)	GCSE	Mean	1.44	0.50	0.00	4.44	2.11
		Std. Dev.	0.88	1.00	0.00	2.24	2.29
(5)	BTEC	Mean	0.00	0.00	0.00	0.83	0.12
		Std. Dev.	0.00	0.00	0.00	0.41	0.33
(6)	CGLI	Mean	0.46	0.00	0.00	0.00	0.14
		Std. Dev.	0.52	0.00	0.00	0.00	0.35
(3)	RSA	Mean	0.00	0.00	0.00	0.37	0.07
		Std. Dev.	0.00	0.00	0.00	0.52	0.25
(25)	Other exams	Mean	3.31	1.25	0.00	0.80	1.37
		Std. Dev.	2.36	1.21	0.00	0.63	1.86
(43)	Other certificates	Mean	1.80	2.00	2.00	1.14	1.79
		Std. Dev.	0.41	0.00	0.00	0.38	0.41

With an average age of about 15 years, it would be expected that the children would be entered for examinations and certificates. The data shows interesting differences among schools. At School 4, GCSE entries were far more frequent than elsewhere. School 1 led in miscellaneous examination entries, while all types of entry were much less frequent at Schools 2 and 3. Schools 1 and 4 thus appeared to be more deeply engaged in the general trend towards a range of levels of certification. By contrast, School 3, where many children had learning difficulties, was represented only in the category of 'other certificates'. It cannot be assumed that there is a uniform pattern of certification among schools possessing the EBD label.

Post-16 and the world of work

Progress in developing future prospects is a key criterion for any school. In 48 per cent of cases children indicated they had known something about job training opportunities a year ago. Sixty-five per cent had improved that knowledge over the past year. Fifty-eight per cent of children knew something about college courses a year ago and exactly the same percentage had improved their knowledge. Care staff reported that only 60 per cent had received career advice in the past year, while 42 per cent completed work experience, mostly for two weeks but the average was just four.

Table 5.13   Average months of post-school education and training already arranged (cases in brackets)

	School 1	School 2	School 3	School 4	No of Cases
Further education (FE)	24.00 (6)	1.00 (1)	12.00 (1)	12.00 (2)	10
Training	0.00 (0)	12.00 (2)	0.00 (0)	0.00 (0)	2

In 18 per cent of cases, post-school education or training had been arranged. Children at School 1 appeared to have longer and more numerous FE placements. Only at School 2 had post-school training placements been arranged. In all, 45 per cent considered they would find a decent job but 33 per cent were unsure. In fact, nine per cent had been offered a job, four per cent permanent full-time and one per cent permanent part-time employment. Post-school education and training were therefore more prevalent than employment. The importance of continued education was emphasised by the fact that 21 per cent had been offered a place for post-16 education at their school. For many of these young people, special education did not stop at 16 years of age, thus extending the school's influence and responsibilities.

Special educational needs

In order to make a general assessment, the areas of individual need identified in each child's statement were translated into specific questionnaire items, on which improvement might have occurred. Because children had varying numbers of assessed needs (up to eight) the improvements were averaged. The table shows how staff and children judged whether or not the areas of special educational need (SEN) displayed improvements.

The range of average improvements identified by the five groups was 55 to 69 per cent, the children's judgements lying midway within that range. Care staff appeared to perceive more improvement that did teachers. The phenomenon of improvement represents a positive attitude to experience

Table 5.14   SEN mean improvement scores over previous year

% improvement	Child		Care staff		Deputy (Care)		Teacher		Deputy (Ed.)	
	No	%	No	%	No	%	No	%	No	%
0–25	9	13	9	13	10	15	14	21	15	22
26–50	21	31	9	13	12	18	12	18	14	21
51–75	14	21	8	12	13	19	20	30	11	16
76–100	21	31	29	43	31	46	21	31	25	37
Mean percentage Improvement	60		69		68		55		61	

over the previous year. In these terms, the data provides some modest encouragement about the direction of change, if not its extent or persistence over the long term. However, they must be set alongside the other data on the curriculum and on emotional and behavioural difficulties which suggest a mixture of successes and hurdles to be overcome. On the SEN measure there were significant differences among the school ratings of care staff and deputy heads (care) with School 4 consistently the most positive. School 2's care staff and School 3's deputy head (care) were the least positive ($p < .01$; $< .05$). Teachers also perceived greater improvements among girls than boys ($p < .05$).

Summary

● The concept of progress used in this study was broad, encompassing a range of social and educational outcomes. The Assessment and Action Record approved for use with children looked after by local authorities influenced the areas covered, the formulation of items, and the general purpose, which was to identify areas of improvement and groups which were benefitting. A cluster of assessments by children, staff and parents was collected, mainly concerned with progress over the past year. The researcher spent a considerable time in preparations for the child interviews.

● We saw how the children were on average 15-years-old at follow-up, having spent an average period of two years eight months at school since admission.

● Seventy-six per cent missed living at home and 58 per cent preferred to live at home.

● For most children, contact and relationships with their parents had been maintained over the past year. Fifty-six per cent reported stable or increased contact with their mothers and 40 per cent with their fathers. Seventy-six per cent reported improved relationships with mothers and 66 per cent with fathers.

- All parents responding to a questionnaire had visited the school in the previous year. Fifty-one per cent wished to visit more often, 46 per cent had received a home visit and 37 per cent wished staff to visit more often. Parents also mostly reported improving relationships with their children.

- Though three-quarters of the children had at least three good friends outside school, 22 per cent had just one or two, or none at all.

- Out of four possible questionnaire responses concerned with feeling personally supported, ten per cent of children gave only one positive response, but the average for them all was over two.

- Fifty-five per cent of children considered themselves treated fairly at school, a feeling especially found among children from minority ethnic groups.

- A large majority of parents had favourable opinions about the schools.

- Children from minority ethnic groups were less likely than other children to report stable or improved contact with other members of their ethnic group.

- In 21 per cent of cases there was a report by school staff of suspected or confirmed abuse over the previous year.

- While 27 per cent had, at admission, at least one health impairment, 42 per cent had at least one reported health impairment at follow-up.

- Sixty-four per cent had at least one medical examination at admission compared with 72 per cent at follow up. However, 30 per cent received no dental examination or only one in the past year.

- Children ranked in order of prevalence the following emotional and behavioural difficulties: nail biting (67 per cent), frequent swearing (45 per cent) and making trouble in class (40 per cent). For staff the main problems were frequent swearing, disobedience at home and lack of concentration.

- Table 5.15 illustrates how the prevalence of some behaviours differed in the documents at admission, compared with currently.

When the behaviours recorded at admission were compared with those reported currently by staff, it appeared that a significant proportion of children were showing more signs of compliance at home and in school. But the rates of offending and sexual exploitation (taking advantage of a partner) had increased.

Table 5.15 Change in EBD

	Admission %	Follow-up %
Non-compliance at home	73	46 (care staff perception)
Non-compliance in school	85	34 (teachers' perception)
Offences in previous year	6	15
Sexual exploitation	6	25 (deputy head – care)

- Ten per cent of children rated themselves as having no emotional or behavioural difficulties, compared with similar ratings of nine per cent by care staff and 16 per cent by teachers.
- One third of the sample had left school without permission on at least one occasion in the previous year.
- Ten per cent of the sample had been excluded from the residential school during the year.
- Children felt their self-control was improving more than did care staff.
- There were significant differences among the schools in children's experiences of being given responsibility and trust.
- While many children showed a wide range of self-care skills, 22 per cent said they could not work out the cost of a dinner in a cafe.
- Children at schools with higher levels of self-care skills and social presentation were also more likely to be entered for examinations and standard educational certificates. More of them also received academic support in the home and did homework.
- Data on basic educational skills and National Curriculum assessments proved difficult to collect.
- Forty-six per cent of children said they had improved in over half the National Curriculum subjects, compared with teachers' assessments of 21 per cent improving to the same extent in attitude and 26 per cent in performance. Teachers and children in the schools influenced by behavioural approaches appeared more positive than those in other schools.
- Twenty-one per cent of the children had been offered a place in post-16 education at the school.
- Eighteen per cent had arrangements for post-school further education or training.
- Children and staff identified average improvements over the previous year in all individual areas of special educational need at between 55 and 69 per cent.
- Teachers perceived greater improvements in these individual areas of need among girls than among boys.

6 Discussion

The themes identified by the study have a general relevance to previous research as well as to current policy and practice. The task of this final chapter is to examine, first of all, the issues raised by the **referral** of children to the variety of services in existence before considering how **school effectiveness** can be conceived and what, in sum, research tells us about the **progress** of children with emotional and behavioural difficulties. Finally, the policy implications of the study need to be drawn out. In the first instance, however, we need to look more closely at the system of services for all children with EBD. It is important to achieve a greater understanding of the place of residential EBD schools within a network of provision run by a variety of agencies.

The agency network

One significant recent approach to the issue of 'difficult' children has sought to identify the common problems of children dealt with by a variety of services such as health, education, social services and so on. The theory argues that, while services have their own definitions, procedures and rhetorics, the young people face a range of shared difficulties and their careers in forms of residential care depend largely on contingencies – for example, which service is contacted and when (Malek, 1991). One implication is that children's needs may be inadequately assessed and met by one service acting largely on its own. One episode of failure may be followed by another, and so on.

There has, for example, been a substantial proportion of 'difficult' children in residential care run by social services (Department of Health, 1992). One study of children's homes found the proportion to be a third, mainly adolescents presenting serious control problems in the home rather than the community (Berridge, 1985). Non-school attendance and behaviour problems in school affected significant minorities of that sample, while a small proportion had attempted suicide. A similar picture emerges from studies of residential assessment facilities (Parker, 1988;

Grimshaw and Sumner, 1991). Historically, a rise in the proportion of children with behavioural difficulties in 'voluntary care' arrangements has occurred – a group, incidentally, significantly represented in the present study sample (Bebbington and Miles, 1989).

There is evidence that parents' complaints about young people's difficult behaviour have been the starting point for many admissions to psychiatric facilities. Such cases have also included non-attendance at school – a significant point for the present study (Jaffa and Dezsery, 1989). Indeed, 11 per cent of psychiatric admissions in one study were referred by educational psychologists. Aggression, difficulties at school and at home, and peer group problems were frequently perceived at admission (Malek, 1991). These were precisely the most frequent characteristics identified in the formal documentation of admissions to residential special provision in the present study. Though suicidal and unhappy feelings were also significantly present among the psychiatric admissions, difficult behaviour was a common finding (Beedell and Payne, 1988). It is clear that some services run by one agency have been used to substitute for services run by another agency which are overstretched or unavailable (Malek, 1991).

On the other hand, it is not a simple question of children experiencing alternative provision for similar problems. There is also evidence to show that young people entering one type of provision have experienced a variety of contacts with different services. This has happened within a single agency domain (Berridge, 1985) as well as among the domains of different agencies. Some services have operated as 'safety valves' for others, as in the case of children with statements of special educational need who have entered psychiatric facilities. As the present study also indicates, this movement can take place in the opposite direction with children in psychiatric care entering EBD schools (Malek, 1991). Social services have also sought placements in the EBD sector for a proportion of children whom they look after.

If we now turn to educational services it is important not to overlook mainstream boarding provision. It is perhaps not widely known that boarding schools represent another possible placement for children with difficulties. It appears from the survey by Anderson and Morgan (1987) that there were substantial proportions of children with a range of special needs, including behaviour difficulties, in privately funded placements at independent boarding schools (p19, Table 2). The children in these categories who receive public financial support appeared very thinly spread over the independent schools. Family difficulties were another reason for placement cited by respondents to that survey, though the degree of support for this category appears to be rather higher. The same thin sprinkling was observed in the maintained sector. Family problems were apparently a growing factor in referrals to maintained sector provision where behaviour difficulties were also noted in a recent report (HMI, 1990).

However, though children in different settings display common problems, a residential special school placement can be obtained, in principle, only through a specific administrative procedure, governed by law. Research shows this to be a lengthy process. Often an assessment can also foreshadow a substantial period in a residential school, as we have seen. How do some children pass through this scrutiny and enter residential schools and others do not, but enter other educational provision? Many children, for example, are excluded from school but do not go on to special schooling. In order to understand the process, a tentative model can be put forward which attempts to grasp how perceptions of difficult children in schools are translated into action.

The labelling process for children with emotional and behavioural difficulties

It is not possible to produce a general theory on the basis of a single study. Evidence about the allocation of large groups of children to different services was not available. However, the case study evidence does point to certain conditions that appear to be necessary before a placement can take place. Based on the findings of the present study, therefore, a theoretical model of the different routes through the educational system would suggest two major alternative paths with different preconditions. One has been the special educational route – the more coherent of the two. Here there is a process of assessment which mainly involves parents, schools and psychologists. While each has its own particular way of construing a child's problems, the point is that, in specific cases, they have in effect coincided. The child with confirmed special educational needs receives labels not from one source, but several. As the data on referrals showed for many cases, the label of 'problem child' is typically corroborated by the parents, the school and perhaps most powerfully by the psychologist. Problems of control were highly prevalent and not confined to one setting alone. Not every child with behavioural problems conforms to this pattern but a significant number do.

How does this come about? From the parents' perspective, it is clear that a number of agencies have confirmed parents' perceptions, albeit without resolving the problems. Apart from the school, many children were in contact with specialist services and clinicians. Parents saw schools and services as potentially useful but frequently felt that more help was necessary which might have prevented a referral to a residential placement. It appears that parents were the weaker participants in the labelling process, corroborating difficulties, agreeing to specialist referral, but not figuring prominently in formal discussions, such as case conferences.

Within the educational system the plausibility of the parent's label is enhanced if, despite any difficulties, the parental household appears to have avoided breakdown, as many in the research appeared to have done. The child's behaviour problem can therefore be perceived as distinctive and, importantly, not adequately explained by environmental stresses. It is at this point that the school label and the parent's label combine, preparing the way for psychological labels. Parents are, in effect, accorded a degree of respectability, rather than sharply challenged. This further assumes that the school is not responsible for the problem, though, as we saw, mainstream strategies were not systematically applied. For the large proportion of children already in special education at admission to a residential EBD school, the 'special' label appears to be a powerful influence. To have special educational needs is to display some consistent difficulties that attract similar labels from more than one key source.

It is also usually assumed that assessment is about securing some form of individual provision. In this sense the application of the label inevitably carries with it some assumptions about appropriate provision from which it is hoped the child may secure benefit. There is an administrative optimism about the assessment process in the sense that it foreshadows some purposeful change of educational arrangements. The special educational route brings together the labels used in the home, the school and by the psychologist. Regrettably, the contribution to the process of children themselves was frequently not recorded, suggesting that the labelling process in effect has excluded them, contrary to the intentions of the Children Act 1989.

The second major alternative path for such children differs from the special educational route. Here, it can be suggested that the labelling process has not been so straight forward. Indeed, the second path is very much the reverse of the medal, compared with the first. On this second major path through the system we would expect to find a greater number of children whose difficulties were not the subjects of convergent labelling. Instead, the problems they pose have normally been seen as situational or environmental, whether those are felt to be rooted in the home or the school. Environmental stresses would be identified that might be the responsibility of other agencies. Or some specific situation in school would be blamed for the problem. Though by a broad definition of special educational needs, such children would qualify for that label, their needs apparently fit less well the practical criteria of the formal statementing process.

One complicating feature may be that there is in fact little agreement about the location of the problem. In cases of behaviour difficulty, parents who consistently blame teachers for their children's behaviour are not likely to concur with the school's definition of the problem. The path into formal EBD provision would be hampered, unless they were felt to be failing in their parental responsibility, thus weakening their position. Another important feature is the duration of the assessment process. For younger children with a record of difficulties, assessment may appear especially appropriate. For older children assessment may be virtually too late. For others there may be little sense of an effective way forward – the reverse of the administrative optimism implied by statementing.

Children on the second major path have not been afforded the relatively coherent provision of the special school sector. Instead, their destinations have been varied and indefinite, whether through on or off-site units or home tuition (Mortimore and others, 1983; Ling and Davies, 1984; Scott and others, 1992). It has been argued that government-approved administrative procedures for dealing with disruptive behaviour have given carte blanche to LEAs in making available whatever level of informal provision they see fit (Galloway, 1985). More recently evidence has been gathered indicating significant local variations in provision combined with changes in its general composition – specifically, a decline in off-site units (Lovey and others, 1993). However, there is also evidence suggesting an increase in the numbers within this informal sector (Stirling, 1991). Assessing trends is made difficult by a lack of available statistics but there has been official concern about rising demand and overstretched facilities. Financial changes associated with the scheme for Local Management of Schools have added to the problems (Ofsted, 1993).

The relationship between exclusion and formal EBD provision illustrates the existence of different paths through a system. In a Sheffield study, it was found that only about 10 per cent of excluded children moved on to special schools. Others entered alternative or mainstream provision (Galloway and others, 1982). It appeared that children in primary schools, in this case, were more likely to end up in special schools than older children, many of whom were too old to be suitable for protracted assessments. Moreover, not all children with EBD have been excluded, as we saw. Exclusion has often followed several public violations of the school's social order. Yet the EBD classification also embraces some children who are perceived as timid and withdrawn (Nottinghamshire County Council, 1990).

Nor have these two major paths been dealt with in an organised manner. Surprisingly, the school exclusion rate was found in one wide-ranging study to have no significant link with the general rate of EBD statementing (Peagam, 1991) nor even with the extent of unit provision! This finding tends to confirm a separation between statementing and exclusion, and indeed between LEA controlled procedures, such as statementing, and school-controlled procedures, such as exclusion. These organisational and administrative factors have clearly been of great weight at the 'macro-level', while the present study concentrates on the 'micro-level'.

The preliminary results of the most recent National Exclusions Reporting System showed that five per cent of excluded pupils had subsequently gone to a special school or changed special school, 22 per cent were in special units, and the rest were either receiving home tuition or in another mainstream school (DFE, 1992). These national figures tend to confirm what more specific studies have found.

All this suggests that children have not arrived in residential EBD special schools by a process of rational assessment and planned allocation. A network of agencies exists with different capacities and approaches. The process of labelling is not straightforward nor does it give evident weight to establishing fully the views of parents and children though parents are often treated as worthy of respect. The results of the present study do nonetheless suggest some of the preconditions for labelling children as having EBD. In the absence of rigorous criteria for residential school placement, the labelling process serves to be make the case for admission.

Systems and the search for effectiveness

It is clear that the systems and practices of residential EBD schooling have developed from a particular history in which a variety of basic concepts have been influential. One of the schools in the study had in fact a long history of dealing with children considered difficult and its past reflected those changes. In particular, the schools in the research currently represented distinct versions of psychotherapy and behavioural treatment as well as different curriculum options. In the case of one school it was evident that a deliberately eclectic approach prevailed. It is worthwhile examining how far historical changes have produced a coherent set of school systems.

The idea of a therapeutic education in a residential setting presented itself as a major advance on the existing practice of residential education which had been dominant in the 19th century. Reformatory schooling was based on assumptions about the influence of moral education and the need to rescue children from evil influences. The form of education and care was also pervaded by assumptions about a fixed social order in which deference to superiors and a spartan lifestyle were supposed to go hand in hand. Punitive thinking joined together theology, social beliefs and moral disciplines in enforcing a unified vision of order (Wills, 1971). The development of disciplined schooling for the unruly assumed that vigorously supervised routines would teach self-control. Yet critics who favoured a therapeutic approach were quick to accuse disciplined schools of presenting a facade behind which violent subcultures flourished (Rose, 1990).

Much of the early work with children considered difficult was inspired by individualistic figures who created idiosyncratic environments for children (Bridgeland, 1971). At the same time children's problems were poorly defined. Since this work took place in independent schools, the 'pioneers' were free to choose cases they felt appropriate to their environment. In practice, the schools' populations tended to be catholic, but the common factor was the perception that the children had been deprived of important experiences, and the schools claimed to provide restorative care. Residential settings were an intrinsic part of the therapeutic design. It was not until 1929 that education authority provision for accommodating children began to include children with difficult behaviour (Bridgeland, 1971).

Accounts of early therapeutic education describe the mystery, fascination and charm through which charismatic individuals exerted influence over children (Rose, 1990). Much of this potency was acquired through reflection and experience but it also became possible to theorise significant personal encounters in a formal psychodynamic manner. The intellectual influence of psychoanalysis became pre-eminent (Bettelheim, 1950; Dockar-Drysdale, 1990; Balbernie, 1966). Therapeutic practice drew on the strength of child guidance in which a medical model held sway. The administrative and legal frameworks of the time defined a concept of maladjustment in precisely these terms (Laslett, 1983).

Much of the therapeutic help given to children with behaviour problems was designed to relieve their emotional and social discomfort. Far less attention was paid to strategies for educating them, according to a new generation of critics. This imbalance was due to the opinion that children's ability to benefit from education was dependent on their emotional and social adjustment (HMI, 1989). Hence, the fundamental problem had been seen as adjustment. The idea that educational progress could be therapeutic took some while to gain influence but it did so as psychologists, rather than psychiatrists, came to exercise more power over referrals. More specific and focused methods were adopted, among them a range of approaches based on behavioural ideas (Cave and Maddison, 1978; Yule, 1982; Herbert, 1987).

The regime ushered in by the Education Act 1981 put 'learning difficulty' at the forefront of concerns about children. Children with EBD were therefore defined with reference to their access to education. Educational psychologists were to be dominant in determining a child's educational needs although the process of determining provision was less clear-cut (Laslett, 1983). The history of provision therefore shows how the accumulation of influential ideas occurred. The psychotherapeutic and behavioural strands were revealed side by side in the Schools Council surveys at the end of the 1970s (Wilson and Evans, 1980; Dawson, 1980). As the present study reveals, they have clearly survived into the present, therapeutic facilities co-existing with behaviourally influenced schools. Equally, there has been a more detached interest in 'effective schooling' which has led to the adoption of the more eclectic methods also found in the present study.

The idea of effective schooling is, in its specific form, comparatively recent. At the same time as the law of special education changed, a considerable interest in 'school effectiveness' had developed (Rutter and others, 1979; Reynolds and Sullivan, 1987). The same principles were applied to approved schools and special education more generally (Millham and others, 1979; Ainscow, 1991). The new emphasis on measuring change and progress was consistent with a more purposeful framework of ideas in special education. But studies of the residential EBD sector did not emerge into prominence until very recently (Cooper, 1993). Nonetheless, the school effectiveness movement was important in suggesting that schools could encourage children to achieve a higher level of results and that difficulties at admission were not the sole reason for poor performance. Indeed, the studies identified key features of schools that were associated with positive outcomes. These can be summarised as follows:

- effective leadership and management;
- a clearly understood focus of instruction;
- praise and responsibility given to pupils;
- a broad and balanced curriculum;
- adequate resources;
- measurement of outcomes. (see Ainscow, 1991)

Specific requirements for dealing with EBD were identified in a survey of schools by Dawson (1980). Especially important in the opinion of schools, were:

● warmth and caring;
● improvement of self-image through success.

These two elements related to both psychotherapeutic and behavioural tasks. More significantly, they also related to widely accepted purposes of good boarding school practice in general. In this sense they helped define a common basis for acceptable professional practice throughout the residential school sector. As Dawson (1980) showed, the characteristic interventions associated with behaviourism or psychotherapy were regarded as effective with specific groups in the schools. For example, psychotherapy suited the 'neurotic' child and discipline the 'conduct disordered'. The way was clear for more deliberately eclectic approaches to emerge. The results of the survey thus could be understood as foreshadowing a set of common standards, as the movement for school effectiveness had also begun to do, but further empirical evidence was slow to arrive.

Key questions still surround the evident variety of school approaches. Although we know a great deal about their origins, it is less easy to see why they have been sustained in such diverse forms. In part, the Education Act 1981 in separating assessment of need from provision made it difficult for referring professionals to be demanding. The monitoring of placements has also become less intensive (Cornwell, 1987). But the evidence of this present study shows one other major reason – the autonomy of heads and school managers. Few other influences appeared to be as powerful in shaping policy and practice. Neither LEAs, governors, parents nor pupils exercised appreciable power. The leadership of schools was able to construct what one Head described as a 'total school ethos' with comparative freedom. The physical distances from referring LEAs seemed also to have restricted the process of monitoring. Crucial issues therefore remained within the power of Heads to decide. We saw, for example, how the issue of physical restraint was an important and difficult one in all schools. In one school in particular, a policy on control had been set which had not been questioned until the Head himself, aware of Children Act 1989 guidelines, initiated discussions among the local education authority and social services. A local inspection of the school then ensued. The use of time out also raised critical questions which research on institutions has highlighted (Murray and Sefchik, 1992; Swartz and Benjamin, 1982). Routine regulation and monitoring of policy and practice by local agencies was not an evident influence. The schools also differed in the design of the curriculum and in their choice of external examination certificates. The organisation of schools had evidently become more complex, requiring a range of expertise and advice. But something of the idiosyncratic flavour of the 'pioneer' schools still lingered.

The organisational autonomy of schools also had implications for the protection of children. It was disturbing to learn from school staff that some form of abuse was either known or suspected in 21 per cent of cases over the previous year. Though the data do not show where the abuse took place, there is an important issue of organisational responsibility here. Their major placement – the residential school – fell within the sphere of **educational** authorities. The level of training among staff in general was also shown to be not comparable with that recommended in similar social services establishments. The training of teachers was found to contain gaps similar to those highlighted in a recent national survey (Cooper and others, 1990). Without the setting of standards by interdisciplinary bodies, it is difficult to envisage how the complex needs of children can be met in the most appropriate manner. The search for common standards which this research is intended to assist requires consultation among a wide range of informed and experienced professionals. It also requires attention to **children's** role and contribution (Hodgkin, 1993).

The extent to which children are taught to take responsibility and participate in decision making has been clearly associated with effective schooling. Most schools in the study, however, did not possess formal mechanisms for registering children's viewpoints. Nor was group work evident in all of them. Indeed the pattern was somewhat surprising, as group work was heavily emphasised in the 'disciplinarian' School 4 but difficult to identify in the more 'therapeutic' School 2. The consistency of what was offered remained questionable. In School 4, for example, behavioural systems such as the token economy co-existed with the progressive development of positive peer culture, despite the specific reservations of the originators of positive peer culture (Vorrath and Brendtro, 1985, p127, p162). Within a behavioural approach it is also possible to introduce elements of self or group-evaluation (Salend and others, 1992). These would seem to deserve greater exploration. In the long march from the early attempts at rehabilitative schooling, it appeared that experimentation in self-government had fallen by the wayside.

Evidence of progress

In order to examine how the result of the present study relate to what is already known, we have to look first at the general outcomes of emotional and behavioural difficulty, before considering the outcomes of specifically residential provision. There is a well established finding that progress occurs over time in over half the identified cases, though to discover positive progress, outcomes need to be measured years rather than months later (Maughan and others, 1985). The results of the National Child Development Study show the pattern of change over a number of years, using the behaviour ratings of parents and teachers at 7, 11 and 16 years of age. The proportions of those no longer considered to show marked difficulty at a later age were summarised as follows:

At home	between 7 and 16	70 per cent
	between 7 and 11	62 per cent
	between 11 and 16	62 per cent
At school	between 7 and 16	70 per cent
	between 7 and 11	65 per cent
	between 11 and 16	65 per cent

(from Fogelman, 1983)

A substantial rate of improvement is indicated. The proportion of children who remained markedly difficult at each age was only two per cent. The findings of studies that examine the impact of particular interventions reveal a similar picture of progress (Topping 1983; Beedell and Payne, 1988). Specialist referrals appeared not to make a significant difference to progress.

One possible implication of these studies was that children's difficulties were reduced by what was called 'spontaneous remission'. Those who might have been described as 'sick' would recover if left 'untreated'. If this idea were accepted, it would mean that the whole purpose of specialist referral could fall into doubt. However, as a concept, 'spontaneous remission' is questionable. It depends on a medical model of behaviour problems, assuming that there is a considerable difference between receiving 'treatment' and not being 'treated', and also that not being 'treated' means that children receive nothing that is likely to affect their behaviour. Yet, in real life, specialist help with behaviour difficulties is likely to involve a range of rather ordinary measures of guidance and support. In addition, not receiving specialist 'treatment' does not mean children do not receive help and guidance. In fact it could mean the reverse, especially when schools and parents are able to cope with difficult behaviour over the considerable period needed before improvement can be seen.

The key questions about progress are therefore what supports children, enabling them to progress and who can provide that support. The evidence of the present study indicates that the problems presented by the children were perceived at referral as intolerable. It was this that led to a residential placement. A major responsibility was thus shifted to a specialist form of intervention. Since other strategies had not been applied systematically it is doubtful whether allocation to a specialist facility had been a fully rational decision. The principal factor seemed to be the feeling that particular schools and parents had exhausted their resources – a far more realistic scenario. An illustration of progress in a range of settings, both residential and non-residential, will be helpful in drawing out these points.

A comparison of outcomes in different settings, focusing on 'psychiatric disorder' in children from seven to 13 years of age showed a steady reduction in disturbance among children in all settings (Kolvin and others, 1987). This finding was consistent with the National Child Development Study. However, for a significant proportion, the outcome was poor, even after two and a half years. Some differences in outcome among the various settings were also evident, with ordinary settings apparently performing better than hospital settings, for example. But disturbance remained more intractable in special schools, whether for 'maladjustment' or 'educational subnormality'. Progress was not only more modest in special schools but it also took longer to take place. For those in special schools for the maladjusted, progress was better in the second year than in the first.

There are two basic questions which affect the interpretation of these results: were there differences in the levels of adversity experienced by these groups of children? Were different methods of intervention applied in the various settings? There are clear indications in the authors' analysis that the answer to both questions is 'yes'. Experience of previous treatment, for example, was a particular feature of the group in special schools for the 'maladjusted', as in the present study. In addition, this group also received more casework and group therapy.

Though the level of problematic behaviour among the groups in that study was similar, their histories were different. Transfer to special school seems to have been a consequence of previous 'treatment failure'. It was not necessarily a reflection of underlying disturbance in the child. Indeed the encouraging results of the group in ordinary settings seem incomprehensible unless we conclude that many very difficult children can improve substantially in mainstream settings without specialist assistance of any kind.

What needs to be clarified is the reason for children's staying in ordinary settings. The most plausible suggestion is that schools and parents possessed sufficient tolerance, resilience and resources to cope with the children's problems and to support the children through their difficulties. Children referred to special schools lacked that protective shield. Indeed the authors' analysis in that study points to a similar conclusion. Some parents clearly cope with difficult behaviour that reduces in intensity over a long period. The category includes parents with more resources, as indicated by the proportion of children from non-manual occupational backgrounds whose difficulties have lessened by the age of 16 (Fogelman, 1983, p336). From the study by Kolvin's team, it seems that what schools offered in the way of casework and therapy was a substitute for the ordinary support and guidance that children in mainstream settings were fortunate to receive. Such an interpretation inverts the hierarchy of the medical model, in which treatment is superior to non-treatment. Indeed, it suggests that, if available (an important consideration), the 'natural' support of schools and teachers is one of the best 'medicines'. The effective special school is therefore put into perspective; at best, it takes the place of something that is not offered elsewhere. In the study by Kolvin's team, the special schools performed this function comparatively less well but nonetheless achieved good or moderate progress in 60 per cent of cases over a two and a half year period – results not dissimilar to those of the present study.

Now that the general conditions of progress have been discussed, it is appropriate to re-examine the existing literature on the outcomes of residential EBD provision. In particular, it will be salutary to consider how the present findings agree with studies completed nearly 30 years ago! A number of studies indicate that over a year to 18 months a substantial proportion of children have achieved some progress, in terms of perceived behaviour change (Roe, 1965; Petrie, 1962; Weinstein, 1969). In some important areas the present study repeats this finding though, in the area of offending, a deterioration was observed. However, previous studies of residential treatment for delinquency, across a spectrum of provision and a range of approaches, present a similarly disappointing picture (Cornish and Clarke, 1975; Millham and others, 1978; Millham and others, 1979; Quay, 1987). Children's views have also been found to be significantly positive (Roe, 1965; Lampen and Neill, 1985; Cooper, 1993); parents too have identified patterns of positive change (Roe, 1965; Weinstein, 1969). In many respects the views of parents and children in the present study echoed earlier findings.

A criticism of previous studies, however, is that they have not taken a broad enough view of developmental change, concentrating sometimes narrowly on behaviour or educational issues. Yet an obvious aspect of residential EBD schools concerns the changes they bring to children's contacts with family, friends and community. In addition, children's development in self-care skills, in personal responsibility and so on needs to be monitored if they are to sustain progress into adulthood (Rutter and others, 1990). It is this whole dimension that the Assessment and Action Record adopted in the present study can highlight. The social consequences of residential schooling have been emphasised by Cooper (1993), referring to the respite from family problems experienced by children. The converse of respite is, of course, renewed contact – a finding highlighted by the present research which shows how relationships were maintained (Beedell 1993). Yet these issues were not identified in any forceful way by previous research on school effectiveness (Dawson, 1980).

The future of residential EBD schooling

The consensus of studies, limited as most have been, is that residential EBD schools can achieve results comparable with many ordinary settings that sustain children. Given the problems of adequately substituting for a supportive 'natural' environment, this would be a creditable result. The panoply of specialist intervention is, at best, an artificial substitute for something rooted in other settings with in-built advantages. The argument put forward by Topping (1983) that schools should achieve **more than** the normal rate of change appears idealistic. Even to achieve consistently the target of normal change requires a constant and close attention to a detailed range of outcomes.

In the present study, some differences observed among schools – for example, in self- care skills, social presentation and examination entries – were of major interest. There is room for further analysis of outcomes, but those particular outcomes were significantly associated with a disciplined achievement model. On the other hand, children's sense of responsibility and autonomy was not, relatively speaking, encouraged by this model, according to pupils' assessments. The long term prognosis for children after experiencing behavioural interventions is, again, relatively speaking, not as favourable (Quay, 1987; Wilson and Evans, 1980). The question of instilling personal responsibility therefore remains both important and unresolved, since it may affect long term outcomes.

Looking elsewhere, we see that the problems of family contact experienced by certain children were associated with a psychotherapeutic, developmental model, that had made, paradoxically, a heavy investment in social work skills to deal with children in care. More pointedly, delinquent behaviour at this school was not reduced by its model of personalised care (Cornish and Clarke, 1975). On other outcomes, the model performed rather better.

In some respects, the findings increase the attractions of a new 'systems' model based on the best of the options on offer. Yet there is a danger that the strengths of one approach may be diluted or even contradicted by inclusion of a feature drawn from a contrasting tradition. Searching for the effective school comes to resemble a bonanza lucky dip in which achieving the target of a general improvement can be expected, with several bonuses and booby prizes added for good measure. Similarly, more recent research on school effectiveness has tended to play down the degree of impact made by differences among schools and to question the idea of a consistent and unified school effect (Reynolds, 1991). Hence, school effects may be identifiable but are not as large as was once hoped. Some children, in other words, make a degree of progress, in spite of, rather than because of, their schools.

Since the aim of policy must be to provide consistent standards, it is still important to examine how outstandingly positive outcomes can be understood in relation to particular practices and integrated, as far as possible, into a coherent 'design for living'. This is why descriptions of actual school practice must be incorporated into accounts of progress. More attention needs to be paid to the common core of activities and relationships which constitute the school experience. Indeed the descriptions of school practice in the present study emphasise the importance of everyday interaction and show how it might be further developed, giving more praise and responsibility to children, for example. The social developmental aspects need to be integrated with the traditional basic values of the residential sector, such as good relationships and providing opportunities for success. In similar fashion, the recent study of Cooper (1993), in dealing specifically with family relationships, has added to the more conventional set of values and practices identified by Wilson and Evans (1980).

Perhaps the greatest and most urgent need is to look at the management of school provision as a whole so that the weaknesses and gaps in ordinary settings can be better understood. Referral to residential placement could then be part of a more coherent plan for children rather than 'demand-led' as at present. It should be possible to set targets of achievement for both mainstream and residential provision. As discussed earlier, a comprehensive overview of the residential sector as a whole would contribute to the development of these standards (Utting, 1992). It might also suggest ways in which specialist services (such as behaviour support teams, parent training or home support) could be managed in the wake of the vast reorganisation of education now under way (Holman, 1988). Indeed, this context of change is extremely important for the residential school sector not simply for organisational reasons but because the indicators of 'demand' show a significant upward trend.

Patterns of family deprivation and poor health, combined with weak networks of social support for families, are known to be associated with reported abuse and with difficult child behaviour (Shaw and McKay, 1969; Bebbington and Miles, 1989; Lempers and Clark-Lempers, 1990; Sampson, 1992). Evidence from the United States has shown how the shrinkage of community services has led to an upsurge of such problems (Sampson, 1992). The question of coping with children who present difficulties is therefore not simply one of choosing individual interventions but of social policy in general. Claims about the rising tide of difficult behaviour in schools and elsewhere recently reported in the press can be understood as a growing perception of social problems that appear not to have been tackled. The transfer of children presenting difficulties to special facilities is the culmination of a wider social policy process in which mainstream supports and services for families have been constrained, against a background of increasing disability, behaviour difficulty and deprivation (Rutter, 1991; Rickford, 1993; Kumar, 1993). Unless the issues of policy and practice are more effectively confronted, there is likely to be a continuing build-up of pressure at all points in the system for dealing with 'disruptive children'. Indeed, the new Education Act, in authorising 'pupil referral units', acknowledges these pressures. Proposals for 'secure training schools' tap another vein of anxiety.

We need more evidence about residential schooling in order to produce a rational system. While this study has shown that residential special schools offered some benefits, there appeared to be no process of planned allocation. It was not clear how the existing preventative measures might have helped to stem and channel the flow of referrals effectively. While the Elton Report had much to say about the day-to-day maintenance of school discipline, it had comparatively little to say about the complex problems of children likely to be referred for residential special education (DES, 1989). Grasping the sharp nettle of policy by initiating a programme of information-gathering and consultation has been long overdue, but there are more optimistic signs of an active policy process as research findings, including those from the present study, have become available.

It is time to consider a more balanced approach to residential special education. Residential education fits the principle of partnership with families since it does not place legal conditions or constraints on the type of service families can receive, in particular, those conditions which might alter the legal relationship between parents and children. This is a major positive factor in favour of such schools. A significant proportion of children for whom both schools and parents have limited tolerance and resources can find a setting in which some of the major social and developmental tasks of childhood can be progressed. As long as society is unable or unwilling to make routine support directly available to the most needy parents and schools, residential special education will continue to play its part. But schools need to be managed within an integrated continuum of provision that is capable of responding to problems in a sensitive and appropriate way.

The evidence of this book has therefore raised a series of question marks about the system of providing for children who present difficulties of a particular kind – those we have frequently described as 'non-compliant' or 'disruptive'. With the Education Act 1993, special educational needs assessment and provision are governed by a new code of practice. It is essential that future policy and practice are based on an expanding body of research evidence. In what ways can the present findings help to define this new agenda for change?

It is important to review regularly the extent to which services capable of preventing and reducing problems of behaviour are available to deal with children's needs promptly and appropriately. Services that address deprivation must enter into this equation. A responsibility for primary prevention also rests on mainstream schools. Organising individual support that includes family needs is a matter for a more complex management strategy that brings together different agencies and professional disciplines. As schools attain greater independence under the new Education Act, it will be essential to make sure that they have sound policies on the primary prevention of behaviour problems and are able to call on a range of services to provide a secondary 'back-up' (Galvin and others, 1990). Under the Children Act 1989, these are certainly children 'in need' entitled to a coordinated response from the agencies within local authorities. The various agencies, working together, need to take a broad overview of service requirements and be able to assess their effectiveness against the costs of providing little or no help. There are calls, for example for a unified system of child mental health services (Light and Bailey, 1993). If such a system was to be set up in one major domain, such as the health service, what would be the consequences for other agencies? There is a critical need to establish a framework of general coordination. Otherwise children may be left to the uncertainties of short-sighted, 'market-biased' decisions by schools that have no great expertise in behaviour problems and do not have to face the consequences for individuals of their decisions. The key principle must be that the costs of not dealing effectively with behaviour problems are communicated to all concerned. It is vital that the local education authority itself is informed of the costs to other agencies of poor decision-making. In this field the argument for interagency coordination is unassailable.

A central feature of any new dispensation must be a better specification of assessment, as recent government proposals have acknowledged. In practice an accumulation of labels occurs, convincing key decision-makers that there is a real problem. It is necessary, in future, for any description of behaviour problems to be specific and to be related to situations and relationships. There should always be consultation with the child, as the Children Act 1989 suggests. It should be clear what kind of emotional problems, if any, are involved. Moreover, it is important that the assessment make clear reference to other children's situations and behaviour, so that we discover in what sense an individual child's behaviour is perceived to present special problems. There may be advantages in producing profiles that allow for ready comparisons, not merely with children in normal classes but also with those in other forms of provision (HMI/Audit Commission, 1992b). Promoting consistency of assessment is an essential task requiring strategic oversight from interdisciplinary bodies. Assessment must also take on the task of identifying, in partnership with parents, what may be hindering the family from giving an appropriate level of support. Again there may be a range of issues to confront but these should be specified wherever possible.

The concept of a child's need for provision requires close attention, in the same vein. Information must be available about the reason for requesting a form of special provision bearing in mind that similar children may be coping adequately in other forms. Here the guiding principles should be that children should be helped in the ordinary setting of their home and community – a point reinforced by the Children Act 1989. However, it should be acknowledged that this can mean a considerable investment for the most needy children and that new packages of services will often need to be invented. A boarding placement could then take its appropriate place in a continuum of services. A local body, with the brief of giving strategic oversight, should be able to establish what form this continuum might take.

Placements in a boarding setting are difficult to review because the placement itself influences the scope of what future options can be explored; for example, it is not at all easy to propose a 'half-way house' when a child is placed miles from home. It may also become difficult to be sure what exactly constitutes 'home' for some children. Continuity of education becomes then a primary argument in favour of maintaining the status quo. It will be important to ensure that home circumstances are properly reviewed, based wherever possible on evidence of children's regular home visits (which themselves require proper resourcing). According to recent government proposals, the local educational authority will have a strengthened responsibility to conduct effective reviews. However, it is important to remember that, in this sector in particular, families may not find it easy to argue their point of view. There seems to be no specialised independent network of help or advice for families, equivalent to that provided by charitable organisations dedicated to other types of need.

One further way of developing the review system would be to clarify the responsibility for overseeing a child's career. A person qualified in special educational needs could act effectively as case coordinator and a personal advocate for the child, managing the links between families and agencies. A panel of these advocates could be appointed for each school, drawing on some staff as well as independent workers in the localities of the boarding school and, wherever possible, the referring agencies. This system might give impetus to the consideration of new options and alternatives, including preparation for leaving school and for a transition to other services. However, it would need careful evaluation before being introduced.

It has become evident that the management of residential special schools needs further attention. A useful role could be played by a local interagency panel in evaluating school policy statements and improving staff training and recruitment to levels comparable with other residential provision for the disadvantaged. All teachers must also have undergone training in special educational needs and have regular access to mainstream school practice. Given the imbalance in gender and ethnicity among children, there is a need for enhanced Equal Opportunities monitoring. Panels of independent visitors may provide a useful sounding board for children. Such arrangements could help to incorporate the schools more effectively in a spectrum of provision including mental health services and social work. It would then be possible to speak of a whole sector of activity with disadvantaged children, in which children's careers could be planned, reviewed and monitored.

In addition to efficient local arrangements for cooperation and evaluation there is a strong case for national regulation and oversight. It should be possible to put the standards applied in all residential settings on a common basis, so that issues in the organisation of daily practice, such as the choice of therapy, or the use of physical restraint, are rationalised. The occurrence of abuse among children in the residential EBD special schools suggests that procedures for identifying and dealing with it must be closely specified. There need to be effective procedures for expert audit and inspection that investigate, for example, whether certain therapeutic practices are properly implemented and with what results. Part of this task will be to see that admissions policies are clear and appropriate; another will be to ensure that appropriate forms of consultation, such as school councils, are in place. A major contribution would be to improve the collection of statistics so that the network of schools and referring agencies could be better understood and the population of special schools might be more accurately determined. On this basis it would be possible to plan adjustments in the provision of schools, rather than to wait for financial crises to force changes.

Finally, if the volume of concerns currently expressed about child behaviour is to be regarded as more than token, there would be little doubt that these issues would rise up the policy agenda and be translated into an energetic search for improvements. For the sake of the children in this book, and many others like them, such a development would be enormously welcome.

References

Ainscow, M 'Effective schools for all: an alternative approach to special needs in education' *in* Ainscow, M. ed. (1991) *Effective Schools for All*. David Fulton

Ainscow, M and Muncy, J (1989) *Meeting Individual Needs in the Primary School*. David Fulton Publishers

Anderson, E W and Morgan, A L (1987) *Provision for Children in Need of Boarding/Residential Education. Research Summary*. Boarding School Association

Association of Child Psychotherapists/The Child Psychotherapy Trust (1992) *Child Psychotherapy: a case for organised funding of training and expansion of the service within the NHS*

Bagley, C (1976) 'Behavioural deviance in ethnic minority children – a review of published studies', *New Community, 5.3, 230-238*

Balbernie, R (1966) *Residential Work with Children*. Pergamon Press

Bamford, F and Wolkind, S (1988) *The Physical and Mental Health of Children in Care: research needs*. Economic and Social Research Council

Barratt, C (1989) *Residential Care: a handbook for newly appointed staff in settings for children with emotional and behavioural difficulties*. Association of Workers for Maladjusted Children

Bebbington, A and Miles, J (1989) 'The background of children who enter local authority care', *British Journal of Social Work*, 19, 349-368

Beedell, C (1993) *Poor Starts, Lost Opportunities, Hopeful Outcomes*. The Charterhouse Group

Beedell, C and Payne S (1988) *Making the Case for Child Psychotherapy: a survey of the membership and activity of the Association of Child Psychotherapists*. Association of Child Psychotherapists

Berridge, D (1985) *Children's Homes*. Basil Blackwell

Bettelheim, B (1950) *Love is Not Enough: The treatment of emotionally disturbed children*. The Free Press

Bone, M and Meltzer, H (1989) 'The Prevalence of Disability Among Children', *OPCS Survey of disability*, Report 3. HMSO

Bowman, I 'Maladjustment: a history of the category' *in* Swann, W ed. (1981) *The Practice of Special Education*. Basil Blackwell

Brannan, C, Jones, J R and Murch, J D (n.) *Castle Hill Report. Practice Guide*. Shropshire County Council

Bridgeland, M (1971) *Pioneer Work with Maladjusted Children. A Study of the Development of Therapeutic Education*. Staples Press

Brown, G W and Harris, T (1978) *Social Origins of Depression*. Tavistock

Cairns, D and Cairns, B The sociogenesis of aggressive and antisocial behaviours, *in* McCord J ed. (1992) op cit

Cave, C and Maddison, P (1978) *A Survey of Recent Research in Special Education*. NFER

Cherlin, A J and others (1991) 'Longitudinal studies of effects of divorce on children in Great Britain and the United States', *Science* 252, 7 June 1991 1386-1389

Cliffe, D and Berridge, D (1991) *Closing Children's Homes, An End to Residential Childcare?* National Children's Bureau.

Cole, T (1986) *Residential Special Education*. Open University Press

Cooper, P (1993) *Effective Schools for Disaffected Students. Integration and Segregation*. Routledge

Cooper, P, Upton, G and Smith, C (1991) 'Ethnic minority and gender distribution among staff and pupils in facilities for pupils with emotional and behavioural difficulties in England and Wales', *British Journal of Sociology of Education*, 12,1, 77-94

Cooper, P, Smith, C and Upton, G (1990) 'Training for special educational needs: qualifications and training requirements of teachers in schools for pupils with emotional and behavioural difficulties in England and Wales', *British Journal of Inservice Training*, 16.3, 188-195

Cornish, D B and Clarke, R V G (1975) *Residential Treatment and its Effects on Deliquency*. Home Office Research Studies 32. HMSO

Cornwell, N (1987) *Statementing and the 1981 Education Act. The Process Of Decision Making*. Cranfield Press. Department of Social Policy, Cranfield Institute of Technology

Coulby, D and Harper, T (1985) *Preventing Classroom Disruption. Policy, Practice and Evaluation in Urban Schools*. Croom Helm

Davie, R, Butler, N and Goldstein, N (1972) *From Birth to Seven: a report of the National Child Development Study*. Longman/National Children's Bureau

Davies, J and Landman, M (1991) 'The National Curriculum in special schools for pupils with emotional and behavioural difficulties: a national survey', *Maladjustment and Therapeutic Education*, 9.3, 130-135

Davies, L (1984) *Pupil Power, Deviance and Gender in School*. Falmer Press

Dawson, R L (1980) *Special Provision for Disturbed Pupils: a survey*. Macmillan Education

Deem, R (1984) *Coeducation Reconsidered*. Open University Press

Department for Education (1992) *Exclusions: a discussion paper*.

Department of Education and Science (1978) *Report of the Committee of Enquiry into the Education of Handicapped Children and Young People*. HMSO

Department of Education and Science (1989) *Discipline in Schools*. Report of the Committee of Enquiry chaired by Lord Elton. HMSO

Department of Health (1991) *The Children Act Guidance and Regulations. Vol 4. Residential Care*. HMSO

Department of Health (1992) *Choosing with Care. Report of the Committee of Inquiry into the Selection, Development and Management of Staff in Children's Homes*. HMSO

Department of Health (1993) *Guidance on Permissible Forms of Control in Children's Residential Care*.

Dockar-Drysdale, B (1990) *The Provision of Primary Experience, Winnicottian Work with Children and Adolescents*. Free Association Books

Docking, J 'Elton's four questions: some general considerations' *in* Jones N ed. (1989) *School Management and Pupil Behaviour*. Falmer Press

Driver, G 'Classroom stress and school achievement: West Indian adolescents and their teachers' *in* James, A and Jeffcoate R, (1981) *The School in the Multicultural Society*. Harper and Row

Farrington, D (1992) 'Exploring the beginning, progress and ending of antisocial behaviour from birth to adulthood', *in* McCord J ed. (1992) op cit

Ferri, E (1976) *Growing up in a One-Parent Family: a long-term study of child development*. NFER

Fogelmann, K (1983) *Growing up in Great Britain. Papers from the National Child Development Study*. National Children's Bureau/Macmillan

Ford, J Mongon, D and Whelan, D (1982) *Special Education and Social Control, Invisible Disasters*. Routledge and Kegan Paul

Galloway, D (1985) *Schools, Pupils and Special Educational Needs*. Croom Helm

Galloway, D and others (1982) *Schools and Disruptive Pupils*. Longman

Galvin, P Mercer, S and Costa, P (1990) *Building a Better Behaved School*. Longman

Garnett, L (1992) *Leaving Care and After*. National Children's Bureau

Gemal, B (1993) 'Factors influencing decisions about placement of children with emotional and behavioural difficulties', *Therapeutic Care and Education*, 2.2., Summer 295-312

Gillborn, D (1990) *'Race', Ethnicity and Education – Teaching and Learning in Multi-Ethnic Schools.* Unwin Hyman

Gillham, B ed. (1981) *Problem Behaviour in the Secondary School. A systems Approach.* Croom-Helm

Goacher, B and others (1987) *Policy and Provision for Special Educational Needs. Implementing the 1981 Education Act.* Cassell

Graham, P (1986) *Child Psychiatry: a developmental approach.* Oxford University Press

Grimshaw, R and Pratt, J (1986) 'Counting the absent scholars: some implications for managerial practice arising from a survey of absenteeism in a city's secondary schools', *School Organisation* 6.1, 155-173

Grimshaw, R and Sumner, M (1991) *What's Happening to Childcare Assessment?* National Children's Bureau.

Grunsell, R (1980) *Beyond Control? Schools and Suspension.* Writers and Readers/Chameleon

Gunaratnam, Y and Berridge, D (1990) *Agencies' Attitudes to Proposed Developments at Hilton Grange.* Unpublished report, National Children's Bureau

Hargreaves, D (1967) *Social Relations in a Secondary School.* Routledge and Kegan Paul.

Hargreaves, D H, Hester, S K and Mellor, F J (1975) *Deviance in Classrooms.* Routledge and Kegan Paul.

Herbert, M (1987) *Conduct Disorders of Childhood and Adolescence. A Social Learning Perspective.* Second edition. John Wiley

Her Majesty's Inspectors of Schools (1989) *A Survey of Provision for Pupils with Emotional/Behavioural Difficulties in Maintained Special Schools and Units.* Department of Education and Science

Her Majesty's Inspectors of Schools (1990) *Boarding in Maintained Schools, A Survey. January 1986-March 1990.* Department of Education and Science

Her Majesty's Inspectorate of Schools (1992) *Non-Teaching Staff in Schools: a review.* Department of Education and Science. HMSO

Her Majesty's Inspectors of Schools/Audit Commission (1992a) *Getting in on the Act. Provision for Pupils with Special Educational Needs: the national picture.* HMSO

Her Majesty's Inspectors of Schools/Audit Commission (1992b) *Getting the Act Together. Provision for Pupils with Special Educational Needs. A Management Handbook for Schools and Local Education Authorities.* HMSO

Hodgkin, R (1993) 'Pupils' views and the Education Bill', *Concern*, Autumn 8-9

Holman, B (1988) *Putting Families First: prevention and childcare.* Children's Society/Macmillan

House of Commons (1987) Education, Science and the Arts Committee Session 1986-87, *Third Report, Special Educational Needs: implementation of the Education Act 1981.* Vol 1 HC201-1. HMSO

Jaffa, T and Dezsery, A M (1989) 'Reasons for admission to an adolescent unit', *Journal of Adolescence*, 12, 187-195

Johnstone, M and Munn, P (1987) *Discipline in School. A review of 'causes' and 'cures'.* Scottish Council for Research in Education.

Keise, C (1992) *Sugar and Spice? Bullying in single-sex schools.* Trentham Books

Kelly, L (1992) 'The connection between disability and child abuse: a review of the research evidence', *Child Abuse Review* 1, 157-167

Kiernan, K (1992) 'The impact of family disruption in childhood on transitions made in young adult life', *Population Studies*, 46, 213-234

Kolvin, I and others (1987) 'Seriously disturbed children in special settings and ordinary schools', *Maladjustment and Therapeutic Education*, 5 Summer 65-81

Kumar, V (1993) *Poverty and Inequality in the UK: the effects on children.* National Children's Bureau

Lampen, J and Neill, T (1985) 'A bucket of cold water – a follow up study in a residential special school', *Journal of Adolescence*, 8.3, 271-287

Laslett, R (1983) *Changing Perceptions of Maladjusted Children, 1945 – 1981*. Monograph 2. Association of Workers with Maladjusted Children

Lees, S 'Learning to love. Sexual reputation, morality and the social control of girls' in Cain, M ed. (1989) *Growing Up Good: policing the behaviour of girls in Europe*. Sage

Lempers, J D and Clark-Lempers D (1990) 'Family economic stress, maternal and paternal support and adolescent distress', *Journal of Adolescence*, 13, 217-229

Levy, A and Kahan, B (1991) *The Pindown Experience and the Protection of Children*. The Report of the Staffordshire Child Care Inquiry 1990. Staffordshire County Council

Light, D and Bailey, V (1993) 'Pound Foolish', *Health Service Journal*, 103, 5339 16-18

Ling, R and Davies, G (1984) *A Survey of Off-site Units in England and Wales*. Centre for Advanced Studies in Education. Occasional publication 2. City of Birmingham Polytechnic

Lovey, J, Docking, J and Evans, R (1993) *Exclusion from School. Provision for disaffection at Key Stage 4*. David Fulton Publishers/The Roehampton Institute.

Lunt, I and Evans, J (1991) *Special Educational Needs under LMS*. Institute of Education, University of London

Malcolm, L and Haddock, L (1992) '"Make-Trouble – Get Results". Provision for Girls in Support Services', *Educational Psychology in Practice*, 8.2. July. 97-100

Malek, M (1991) *Psychiatric Admissions: a report on young people entering residential psychiatric care*. The Children's Society

Malek, M and Kerslake, A (1989) *Making an Educational Statement? An analysis of the admission of children with emotional and behavioural difficulties to residential special school*. University of Bath/Children's Society

Maughan, B, Gray, G and Rutter, M (1985) 'Reading retardation and antisocial behaviour: a follow-up into employment,' *Journal of Child Pschology and Psychiatry*, 26, 5, 741-758

McCord, J 'Long-term perspectives on parental absence' in Robins, L N and Rutter, M eds (1990) *Straight and Devious Pathways from Childhood to Adulthood*. Cambridge University Press, 116-134

McCord, J ed. (1992) *Facts, Frameworks and Forecasts. Advances in Criminological Theory Vol 3*. Transaction

Millham, S (1987) 'Residential schools: issues and developments', *Maladjustment and Therapeutic Education*, 5.2, 4-11

Millham, S, Bullock, R and Cherrett, P (1979) *After Grace-Teeth. A Comparative Study of the Residential Experience of Boys in Approved Schools*. Human Context Books

Millham, S, Bullock, R and Hosie, K (1978) *Locking Up Children. Secure Provision Within the Child-Care System*. Saxon House

Mitchell, S and Shepherd, M (1966) 'A comparative study of children's behaviour at home and at school', *British Journal of Educational Psychology*, 36. 248-254

Mongon, D and others (1989) *Improving Classroom Behaviour: new directions for teachers and pupils*. Cassell Educational

Mortimore, P and others (1983) *Behaviour Problems in Schools: an evaluation of support Centres*. Croom Helm

Moses, D, Hegarty, S and Jowett, S (1988) *Supporting Ordinary Schools: LEA initiatives*. NFER-Nelson

Murray, L and Sefchik, G (1992) 'Regulating behaviour management practices in residential treatment facilities', *Children and Youth Services Review*, 14, 519-538

Newth, S (1986) 'Emotional and behaviour disorder in the children of Asian immigrants', *Association for Child Psychology and Psychiatry Newsletter*, 8, 4, 10-14

Northern Examining Association (1990) *Northern Partnership for Records of Achievement: scheme for the accreditation of centres for records of achievement. guidance for schools and colleges*.

Nottinghamshire County Council (1990) *Pupil Exclusions from Nottingham Secondary Schools*. Full Report 15/89

Ofsted (1993) *Education for Disaffected Pupils (1990-92)*. Office for Standards in Education

Ogden, J (1992) 'In the wake of terror', *Social Work Today*, 23, 48, 12-14

O'Leary, S G and O'Leary, K D 'Behaviour modification in the school', *in* Leitenberg H ed. (1976) *Handbook of Behaviour Modification and Behaviour Therapy*. Prentice Hall Inc

Parker, R 'Children' *in* Sinclair, I ed. (1988) *Residential Care. The Research Reviewed*. HMSO

Parker, R and others (1991) *Assessing Outcomes in Child Care. The Report of an Independent Working Party Established by the Department of Health*. HMSO

Peagam, E (1991) 'Swings and roundabouts: aspects of statementing and provision for children with emotional and behavioural difficulties', *Maladjustment and Therapeutic Education*, 9.3 Winter 160-169

Petrie, I (1962) 'Residential treatment of maladjusted children', *British Journal of Educational Psychology*, 32, 27-39

Pumfrey, P N and Reason, R (1991) *Specific Learning Difficulties (Dyslexia): challenge and responses*. NFER/Nelson

Pyke, N (1993) 'Hauling in the lines of support', *Times Education Supplement*, 22 October, 3

Quay, H 'Institutional treatment' *in* Quay, H ed. (1987). *Handbook of Juvenile Delinquency*, John Wiley

Reid, K (1986) *Disaffection from School*. Methuen

Reynolds, D 'When pupils and teachers refuse a truce' *in* Mungham, G and Pearson, G eds (1975) *Working Class Youth Culture*. Routledge and Kegan Paul

Reynolds, D (1991) 'School effectiveness and school improvement in the 1990s', *Association for Child Psychology and Psychiatry Newsletter*, 13.2, 5-9

Reynolds, D and Sullivan, M (1987) *The Comprehensive Experiment*. Falmer Press

Rickford, F (1993) 'Minor disorder', *Social Work Today*, 25, 4. 28 January, 11

Roe, M (1965) *Survey into Progress of Maladjusted Pupils*. Inner London Education Authority

Rose, M (1990) *Healing Hurt Minds. The Peper Harow Experience*. Tavistock/Routledge

Rowe, J Hundleby, M and Garnett, L (1989) *Child Care Now: a survey of placement patterns*. Research Series 6 BAAF

Rutter, M (1966) *Children of Sick Parents: an environmental and psychiatric study*. Institute of Psychiatry, Maudsley Monographs no 16. Oxford University Press

Rutter, M (1972) *Maternal Deprivation Reassessed*. Penguin

Rutter, M (1975) *Helping Troubled Children*. Penguin

Rutter, M (1991) 'Whither child psychiatric services?', Paper given at the Robina Addis Memorial Lecture, at the Young Minds Conference, November 1990.

Rutter, M and Giller, H (1983) *Juvenile Delinquency: trends and perspectives*. Penguin

Rutter, M and Madge, N (1976) *Cycles of Disadvantage*. Heinemann Educational

Rutter, M and others (1974) 'Children of West Indian Immigrants I, Rates of behavioural deviance and of psychiatric disorder', *Journal of Child Psychology and Psychiatry*, 15, 241-262

Rutter, M and others (1975) 'Children of West Indian Immigrants III, Home circumstances and family patterns', *Journal of Child Psychology and Psychiatry*, 16, 105-124

Rutter, M and others (1976) 'Adolescent turmoil: fact or fiction?', *Journal of Child Psychology and Psychiatry*. 17, 35-6

Rutter, M and others (1979) *Fifteen Thousand Hours: secondary schools and their effects on children*. Open Books

Rutter, M, Quinton, D and Hill, J (1990) 'Adult outcome of institution reared children: males and females compared,' *in* Robins, L and Rutter, M eds (1990) *Straight and devious pathways from childhood to adulthood*. Cambridge University Press 135-157

Rutter, M and Quinton, D 'Psychiatric disorder – ecological factors and concepts of causation' *in* McGurk, H ed. (1977) *Ecological Factors in Human Development*. North Holland

Rutter, M, Tizard, J and Whitmore, K eds (1970) *Education, Health and Behaviour*. Longman

Salend, S T, Whittaker, C R, and Reeder, E (1992) 'Group evaluation: a collaborative peer-mediated behaviour management system', *Excep- tional Children*, 59. 3. 203-209

Sampson, R J (1992) 'Family management and child development: insights from social disorganisation theory', *in* McCord, J ed. op cit

Scherer, M (1992) 'Child abuse in a therapeutic community', *Therapeutic Care and Education*, 9, 1.3. 151-163

Scott, G, West A and Varlaam, A (1992) 'Special educational provision for children with emotional and behavioural difficulties', *European Journal of Special Needs Education*, 7.3, 259-272

Shaw, C R and McKay, H D (1969) *Juvenile Delinquency and Urban Areas*. Revised edition. University of Chicago Press

Shaw, O (1965) *Maladjusted Boys*. Allen and Unwin

Smith, A J and Thomas, J B (1992) 'A survey of supportive work with the families of pupils in schols for emotionally and behaviourally disturbed children', *Therapeutic Care and Education*, 1.3, 135-150

Smith, D J and Tomlinson, S (1989) *The School Effect: a study of multi-racial comprehensives*. Policy Studies Institute

Stein, M and Carey, K (1986) *Leaving Care*. Blackwell

Stirling, M (1991) 'Absent with leave', *Special Children*, November 10-13

Stone, M (1983) *Ethnic Minority Children in Care*. A report to the Children in Care Panel, Social Science Research Council

Swann, W (1991) *Segregation statistics. English LEAs. Variations between LEAs in levels of segregation in special schools, 1982-1990*, Centre for Studies on Integration in Education

Swartz, S L and Benjamin, C (1982) *The use of punishment and time-out in a residential treatment program for emotionally disturbed children*. Paper for Conference on Programming for the Developmental Needs of Adolescents with Behaviour Disorders. Minneapolis, Minnesota (ERIC Document 223012)

Tomlinson, S (1982) *A Sociology of Special Education*. Routledge and Kegan Paul

Tomlinson, S (1983) *Ethnic Minorities in British Schools, a review of the literature, 1960-82*. Heinemann

Tomlinson, S (1992) 'Education and training', *New Community* 18(3), 463-468

Topping, K J (1983) *Educational Systems for Disruptive Adolescents*. Croom Helm

Troyna, B and Hatcher, R (1992) *Racism in Children's Lives: a study of mainly white primary schools*. Routledge/National Children's Bureau

Utting, W (1992) 'Broken minds – broken lives', Paper for Charterhouse Group Conference

Vorrath, H and Brendtro, L (1985) *Positive Peer Culture*. Second Edition, Aldine

Weinstein, L (1969) 'Project Re-Ed schools for emotionally disturbed children: effectiveness as viewed by referring agencies, parents and teachers', *Exceptional Children*, 35.9, 703-711

Wills, D (1971) *Spare the Child*. Penguin

Willis, P E (1977) *Learning to Labour*. Saxon House

Wilson, M and Evans, M (1980) *Education of Disturbed Pupils*, Schools Council Working paper 65. Evans/Methuen Educational

Wilson, P (1993) 'A crisis in residential childcare and therapy', *Young Minds Newsletter*, 13, 2-4

Wolpe, A (1988) *Within School Walls, The Role of Discipline, Sexuality and the Curriculum*. Routledge

Wright, C (1986) 'School processes' *in* Eggleston, J, Dunn, D and Anjali, M *Education for Some: the educational and vocational experience of 15-18 year old members of minority ethnic groups*. Trentham Books

Yule, W 'Behavioural treatment of children and adolescents with conduct disorders' *in* Hersov, L and Berger, M eds (1978) *Aggression and Anti-Social Behaviour in Childhood and Adolescence*. Pergamon Press

Yule, W (1984) 'Child behaviour therapy in Britain 1962-1982', *Association for Child Psychology and Psychiatry Newsletter*, 6.1, 15-20

Index

The index covers Chapters 1 to 6. Entries are arranged in letter-by-letter alphabetical order (in which spaces and hyphens between words are ignored for filing purposes). Where an entry contains several page references, any principal reference is printed in bold type.